ADVANCE PRAISE

"This book is a must for any business owner.
It feels like *Entrepreneurial Happiness* contains the best
elements of the top business books, all in one simple
and enjoyable read."

Stuart Milton, Business Owner,
Reservoir Finance

"As accountants and business advisers we would highly
recommend taking time out to explore the principles
contained in this book. The simple exercises are
extremely effective in helping to think 'outside the
box'; stimulating new ideas and strategies that can
have a transformational impact on your business
and your life in general."

Carolyn Frostwick, Accountant,
Philip Daulby Financial Management

Published by
LID Publishing Limited
The Record Hall, Studio 304,
16-16a Baldwins Gardens,
London EC1N 7RJ, UK

info@lidpublishing.com
www.lidpublishing.com

A member of:

BPR ⊛
businesspublishersroundtable.com

Printed by Gutenberg Press, Malta
ISBN: 978-1-912555-81-9

Cover design: Matthew Renaudin
Page design: Caroline Li

ENTREPRENEURIAL
HAPPINESS

How to Build an Abundant
Business and a Fulfilling Life

CHARLIE READING

MADRID | MEXICO CITY | LONDON
NEW YORK | BUENOS AIRES
BOGOTA | SHANGHAI | NEW DELHI

CONTENTS

DEDICATION

I passionately believe that running your own business can give you the most amazing life because, ultimately, you are in control of who you spend your time with, what you spend your time doing and where you spend it. These three choices give you the opportunity to craft the life of your dreams. There has never been a better time to set up your own business, and never been a time when you can take on a multinational corporation from your bedroom until now!

As a result, I would like to dedicate this book to the young entrepreneurs of the world. You can do this, and you can create an amazing life for yourself.

In addition, I'd like to specifically acknowledge a few people:

Ffion and Bronwyn: I hope one day I can help you set up your own businesses doing whatever it is you have a passion for. Thank you for your understanding that I am not perfect at any of this.

Caryl: I hope some of what is in here can help you make an amazing success of your art. It is incredible. Thank you for your support in everything I do.

Mum and Dad: Thank you for your support over the years. Particularly those words of encouragement: "Trying a career in financial services is a bit like turning pro at golf.

If you don't give it a go, you'll never know." It seems to have worked OK so far!

The Efficient Portfolio Team: you guys rock. You continue to strive to better yourselves, our business and how we help our clients. Without you, this couldn't happen.

To all the people who have taken the time to develop courses and write books that I have been able to learn from: specific thanks to The Strategic Coach® Program, my coach, David Batchelor, Andy Harrington, George Kinder and Tony Robbins.

Finally, to all those who read and implement the ideas in this book and go on to create amazing businesses: there is no better reward for a teacher than for his students to surpass his achievements. If I can ever do anything to help you on this journey, please drop me a line at charlie@efficientportfolio.co.uk. I'd love to help.

FOREWORD

By teaching people to grow their visibility, credibility and authority, I get to meet a lot of business owners, and when I chat with them, I see the same concerns time and time again. With few exceptions, most are struggling to generate enough leads for their businesses and, ultimately, enough profit. They are working too many hours and don't have the work-life balance they want. And finally, rather sadly, many of them are falling out of love with their businesses, and they no longer enjoy what they spend most of their time doing.

If you don't generate enough leads, you don't generate enough income for your business. This massively restricts what choices you can make for your business and your life. It restricts how you market yourself, how many people you employ and also how much you pay yourself. I dare say you didn't get into running your own business or being a partner in a bigger business in order to settle for an average life and lifestyle. You did it to create something special for you and the people around you.

If you get your work-life balance wrong – which, let's face it, we've all done at times – it can be even worse than not making enough money. When your balance is off, you stop doing the things that keep you happy and healthy, and that leads to a downward spiral. While you may not see the signs immediately, the effect on your long-term health can be huge. Of course, it isn't just you who suffers. When you are working too many hours, you miss out on spending time with the people you care most about. Whether it's with your significant other, your children while they're growing up, or even your grandchildren, you only get one shot at this life, and once your time has gone, it's gone. Research shows that at the end of their lives, people don't regret not working enough hours or even making enough money; their regrets are centred around the experiences they didn't get to enjoy, and the time they didn't get to spend with people.

When you run your own business, it is so easy to get bogged down in the elements of the business you think you should do, the elements of your day-to-day work that you have to get around to or have no one to delegate to. We all know it is easier to get the job done ourselves than teach someone else to do it, especially with the worry of whether they'll do it as well as we can.

As a result, I see many business owners dreading more and more their life in business. They fall out of love with the work they originally had such passion to deliver. The reason I wrote *Passion Into Profit* is because people generally have a huge drive for change at the start of their business but, over time, if they don't become the go-to person for their industry, the business can fade away.

Over the years, I have come to know Charlie extremely well. We initially met when we were both speaking at the National Achievers Congress, and I am proud to say that I went on to train Charlie in public speaking. He even won an award at our professional speaker's award ceremony that we hold annually. He won that because he is the sort of guy who, when he commits to doing something, makes sure he does it well. He dives right in, quite literally. So much so that I asked him to speak at my event, Power to Achieve. Since then, he has gone on to speak at his industry's global conference in front of 11,000 of his peers. Like I said, he doesn't do things by halves!

What he has achieved with Efficient Portfolio, and how they have differentiated themselves from their competition, is quite remarkable. While I have very little trust for his peers, I have a huge amount of trust and respect for Charlie. Business isn't just about how much money you make; it's about what you do with it, too. While in this book Charlie doesn't really cover much on that subject, he is one of the few people from whom I would seek this advice because his business is at the forefront of the industry.

What Charlie has done in writing *Entrepreneurial Happiness* is refine down all of the best ideas he has uncovered on his road to success. He is humble in giving credit to the sources that he has learned from but, of course, it is in the implementation of these ideas where the real magic happens. Anyone can read a book; it is what you do with it that counts. What I love about this book is that, if you take its advice, follow its strategies and implement its ideas, you have the ability to make more money, keep more of that money, create better health, wellbeing and relationships, all while enjoying life more. What more could you ask for? If you got half as much as that from most books, you'd be delighted.

So, take my advice: read and study this book. The contents are powerful beyond measure. Follow his advice, and you too could create more *Entrepreneurial Happiness* in your life.

Andy Harrington
Sunday Times Bestselling Author
*Passion Into Profit – How to Make Big Money
from Who You Are and What You Know*
(to download a free audio copy, please visit
www.efficientportfolio.co.uk/AndyHarrington)
www.AndyHarrington.com

PROLOGUE

A long-standing client of mine runs a successful carpentry business in the UK; for the purpose of this book, let's call him Joe. Joe is a lovely genuine gentleman, and a real family man who cares deeply for his wife and two children.

Joe worked for a large furniture company in his younger years, but in his 40s, he became disillusioned with the way the company treated their customers and their employees and, like so many people, he saw what was being done wrong and wanted to do it better. He was a good carpenter, very good at design, and he felt that he could create a better product at a better price and provide a better customer experience.

So, halfway through his working life, Joe decided to step into the world of entrepreneurship and set up his own business in the form of Tables R Us. Just a few years later, they were making amazing furniture, delivering a great customer experience, all at a reasonable price, and their customers really valued what they did. They did a particularly brilliant trade in bespoke kitchens, which is where Joe excelled, because his creativity could really shine through and he could engage with the customer and really get to the heart of what they wanted.

Joe loved what he did, and wanted to make the best of his business, not just for himself, but also for his family.

He worked hard throughout his life, but as he aged, he realized that he needed to slow down. He was tired of working long hours and never spending time with his loved ones or pursuing his other passion of golf. With some reluctance, he decided it would soon be time to retire, so Joe wisely started to reengineer Tables R Us so that he could sell the business.

Joe sought out the help of a business coach. With the help of his coach, Joe gradually delegated more of what he did on a daily basis and soon it was finally time to hand over the final piece of the business: the oversight of new product design. This was the part of his job that Joe loved the most, where he excelled, and the differentiator between him and his competitors; in fact, it was the reason he got into the business in the first place.

Joe came to see me at our annual review meeting, where we make sure his financial plan is on track and make changes for the year ahead. Joe's finances were in order, he was ready to retire, and an offer was on the table to sell Tables R Us. We had built Joe a lifetime cash-flow forecast, a tool we use to help our clients visualize what their financial future looks like, so he knew that the offer far exceeded the figure he needed to retire comfortably. If he accepted, he would be financially free for the rest of his life, even if he lived to 100, and that was a great feeling for him. Theoretically, he could now accept the offer and retire happily, sailing off into the sunset. But what Joe said to me next was both shocking and inspiring.

With a tear in his eye, Joe said, "Two years ago I was desperate to get out of the business, and now I have all the money that I need to retire. When I was overworking to keep the business moving forwards, I really wasn't enjoying it. There was a never-ending list of jobs to do, no time to enjoy what I wanted to be doing outside of work, and no future prospect of that changing. Yes, I loved the product design, but as the business grew, I was getting to do that less and less, and I was getting bogged down with the other stuff. The regulations and legislation around our business was where I was needed most, but I hated it.

"So, I should be really excited about selling and retiring, but the problem is, having paid a business coach to help me delegate all of the elements that got me down, recently I've only been doing the parts of the business that I love."

Then came the sucker punch: "So now that I only do the parts I love, I don't know that I want to sell or retire. All I do now is design the products, which I adore. Thanks to the team we've built, I can now work on my terms, as little or often as I want. I can engage with the customers, help them with my wealth of experience, and help them get the furniture and kitchen of their dreams, and I love that, so why would I now sell? I have fallen back in love with my business and my passion. I think I've found the perfect compromise. I can retire, while still keeping one hand in the business, so I think I am going to carry on instead."

This was fantastic for Joe. He could now sail gradually into retirement working as he wanted, and he only had to do the bits he loved and was best at. He had freed up enough time to enjoy his other passions – golf and his family.

And do you know what happened? Not only did he enjoy life more, but his business actually increased in profitability. He was working less, loving life more and making more money. Isn't that what everyone is looking for?

This might sound odd, but instead of being elated for Joe, I was slightly disappointed for him. He had been running Tables R Us for the last 30 years, and only in the final stage of his working life did he figure out how to have the balance he wanted. While money had never been the motivational factor for him, he was now making the kind of income his expertise deserved. Imagine what Joe's life might have been like had he implemented those changes some 20-plus years ago? How much more money would he have made? How much more time could he have spent with his young family? And how much more could he have enjoyed those years?

I thought back to my first meeting with Joe. I had asked him a searching question I ask everyone at our initial meeting. "Imagine you go to see your doctor, and he shocks you with the news that you only have one day left to live. Ask yourself, what would you be thinking about in that 24 hours?" I distinctly remember that one of Joe's regrets was not spending enough time with his children when they were growing up because he had been working so hard.

As a dad myself, it is always saddening to hear that someone has lost that time, because they will never get it back and that time is precious. Sadly, for Joe, he didn't have to sacrifice as much time as he did; he could have achieved everything so much more easily, effectively and been better rewarded if he'd acted sooner.

Had Joe employed the methodology of the business coach many years earlier, he could have seen even more success in his business, while having spent more time with his children as they grew up. Not only that, he would have enjoyed his work so much more.

Hindsight is a wonderful thing, but there is little to be gained by it. I believe in looking forwards, not backwards. Really all that we can do is change things for the better now, and that is what this book is about.

CHAPTER 1

HOW CAN THIS BOOK HELP?

Would you like for your business to be making more money than you know what to do with? What if it was making so much that you were more worried about what you were going to do with it all, rather than when you would make the next breakthrough?

And how would you like to run a business in which you only do the things you love? The time you spend working in the business can be as much or as little as you like, so that you relish your time at work and also have all the free time you need.

If the answer is 'yes' to any of these questions, congratulations on taking the first step in creating your compelling new future.

Do you sit and wonder why you are working harder than you did when you were employed? You may remember thinking that, "If only I ran my own business, I could play more golf, cycle more, travel with my family more and get back into shape," but in reality, you actually have less time now than you ever did. I have no doubt that one of the reasons you liked the idea of setting up your own business was so that you could control your most precious commodity: time. But do you get the time for yourself and your loved ones that you need or deserve?

It's not so many years ago since I was in this same situation with no time to look after myself, to do the things I enjoyed or to spend time with the people I love the most, and it was getting me down. I was successful financially, but what was the point if I couldn't live the life I wanted?

Time is, without doubt, our most precious commodity. Bruce Lee said, "If you love life, don't waste time, for time is what life is made up of. No amount of money or power can buy you more time."

Have you noticed that time just seems to keep getting faster and faster? There is good reason for this. Each year of our lives is a smaller percentage of our total lives than the previous year, so every year will feel quicker than the last. A scary thought, isn't it? If you want to make changes in your life, you'd better get started now, as there is no time to waste. After all, every hour you waste is another hour you will never get back.

Perhaps you're also frustrated that you never seem to make quite as much money as you think your efforts deserve. You are the bottleneck to your company making more money, and you have hit a ceiling that you just don't seem to be able to break through. Maybe your business is going backwards? Or are you trying to compete in the modern world of technology and innovation but never really making progress? Or maybe you're just prolonging the inevitable?

Have you ever woken up on a Monday morning with a certain amount of dread? Maybe you were thinking about the endless, monotonous list of crucial but hated tasks? That long list of jobs that you don't enjoy but if you don't do them will be overlooked. Has the fun drained out of running your own business because you spend too little of your time there pursuing or practising your passion? Instead, are you faced with the bottomless quagmire of 'admin,' such as clearing out your inbox?

If this life of insufficient time, money and enjoyment is where you are at the moment, where would you like to be?

I'd like you to imagine that you now have more money in your business bank account than you are sure what to do with. Money to invest into new projects and ideas, money to reward your team with what they really deserve, and money to create a business environment that you can all enjoy. Your money is not just in the business account, though, because you have a sizeable personal portfolio that means that you are financially free of the business, and you could stop working at any time if you chose. The great thing is that you don't actually want to, because work is now on your terms. Does that sound like a nice predicament?

Imagine that you only work at the elements of the business where you excel, and you absolutely love. The aspect of the business that exemplifies why you set up in the first place; the element that, if it was the only thing you did, you would never 'work' a day in your life. Imagine focusing all your time and energy on that part of the business with no admin. Wouldn't that be amazing?

And that's not the end of it – imagine you also do it on your terms. You only work the number of hours a week, month or year that you want to. You have all the time you need to explore the world with your loved ones, keep fit and healthy and enjoy the other activities you are passionate about. You are in the best shape of your life, travelling to the best places you've ever seen, and creating the best memories with the people around you. Does that sound like an incredibly rewarding life? It certainly excites me.

If what you're doing now is generating little money, creating hassle and devouring your time, wouldn't you agree that you might need a different approach?

Let's face it. We only get to live this life once and, as we've already established, time is slipping away quicker than we think, so we need to get on and do this. Otherwise, we will be one of those people who sits there lamenting the past's possibilities.

I want you to imagine that, many years from now, you are lying on a bed in a clean white hospital room. This isn't just any hospital bed, though; this is your deathbed, and this is your last day on this Earth. And on this day, something incredible happens – another you walks through the door. How do they look? Happier or sadder than you? More or less successful than you? More or less healthy than you?

On this day, in that hospital room, you get to meet the person that you could have become. How do you feel? Are you happy that you didn't become that person or is the opposite true? How awful it would be to meet someone who is far more successful, someone who has had far more fun, and someone who made significantly more money and impact on the world than you. How would you feel, knowing that if you had made different choices, you could have had their amazing life instead? Can you think of anything worse than lying on your deathbed thinking about what could have been, and what you should have done with your life?

This 'stuff' is really important. Whether you get this right or not shapes your whole life – and not just yours. It shapes the lives of the people you love the most. It shapes what adventures they will experience, how much quality time they get to spend with you, and the memories they will make. Could there be a more important subject to study? This impacts everything you can account for at the end of your life, so let's spend some time together improving how we go about it.

You could enjoy your time at work more, have the time to create special memories with those important to you, look after yourself better, and maybe even have more money to create the life you love. Can you really afford to wait on areas of your life that are as important as these? If you want to create this amazing new life for yourself, you need to take action now.

––––––––––

Michael Gerber, author of the brilliant *The E-Myth Revisited: Why Most Small Businesses Don't Work and What to Do About It*, uses the phrase "working *on* your business as opposed to working *in* it." I love this saying, because it sums up how we create a successful business that will lead to entrepreneurial happiness. Most small business owners are so busy working in their businesses, they don't have the time to work on making it better. That impacts their business effectiveness, allows them to continue to make the same mistakes and stops them from reaching their potential. That's what this book is about. It is about identifying how you can work smartly 'on' your business to make it better.

In this book, I will share the secrets and the tools that have helped me achieve this so far in my business, Efficient Portfolio. I share the techniques that you can use and the questions that you need to answer, but only you will have the answers. You have the answers for your life and business within you; you just need someone to ask you the right questions. **You can win the business race, as long as someone gives you the right track to run on.**

In addition to the tools and techniques, there is a hidden message within this book. You may not get it the first time you read it, so you might need to read it more than once to pick up on this subtler point. When you do you will realize that you have even more power within you than you thought. I hope you find it.

I hope this book helps you change your life, and the lives of the people you love the most. I read a lot, and where I am able to, I'll give credit to the sources of my wisdom. This won't always be possible though, as sometimes I cannot recall where I got it from, or it's a blended solution from a variety of sources. If I fail to give credit to anyone or anything that has helped me on my journey, I apologize in advance.

Read it, enjoy it, then action it. A million ideas will change nothing; one purposeful action can change everything!

CHAPTER SUMMARY

- If you don't find Entrepreneurial Happiness, you will miss out on making your business the best it can be.

- You'll also miss out on spending time with the people you care the most about and looking after yourself.

- Finally, when you're at work you'll become demotivated because you aren't actually enjoying what you do.

- Entrepreneurial Happiness is that sweet spot where you are making great money, have a great work-life balance and love the time you spend at work.

CHAPTER 2

MY STORY

You may be wondering, who is Charlie Reading and why should I listen to him? I'd be asking these exact questions, so it's only fair that I give you a bit of background as to where I have come from and how I can help you to achieve time, fun and profit in your business.

Have you ever had a time when you were lost, and didn't know where your future was taking you? If you had been with me on an October evening in 1998, you'd have seen me in the kitchen of my parent's 200-year-old stone farmhouse that was nestled in the heart of the beautiful Rutland countryside.

On that October evening, I was sitting on the huge wooden dresser that was home to Mum's wide array of blue and white crockery. Sitting on the dresser, I said, "Dad, I have had it with farming. It's only been four months since I finished my degree at Newcastle, and I am already being driven crazy by agriculture. I know I have helped you on the farm since I was 15, but that was always a means to an end. This is different now that I've finished my education. There is no end, and I hate it. I cannot spend the rest of my life sitting on a tractor hour after hour listening to Test Match Special and Atlantic 252. If this is all there is to my life, then I want out."

My dad, a smaller, balder, slightly less-good-looking version of me, said, "Charles (my dad is one of the only people to call me by my birth name), don't farm because I did. It is there for you if you want it, and we can diversify into something that interests you more if you wish, but if you don't want to farm, then you need to find something else you want to do. You need to do some serious thinking, but if you do want to step away from farming, that is OK with me, just as long as you do something worthwhile with your life. You only get one shot, after all, and if farming isn't for you, then you need to go and plough your own furrow.

If you work hard at whatever you do, I am sure you will be successful. If you don't give it a go, you'll never know whether you could have made it."

It was at this juncture I thought I'd air an idea. "Kate and I have been together now for over a year, and with her dropping out of university, I think maybe we should go travelling together. Go see the world, and hopefully that might give me some ideas as to what I want to do. I could use the money that Grandad left me in his will. That should last me around six months if I am careful."

Fast forward just a few months, and I am sitting on the pavement in Perth, Western Australia, with Kate. The heat was intense, and so was the atmosphere. We had finished travelling around South Africa, an experience that had expanded my mind. The travelling, the scenery, the culture and my first safari had opened my eyes to a world I had not seen before. But while the travelling had been amazing, our relationship had not. I had found an enthusiasm for exploring the world, culture and nightlife that I had lacked at university, but Kate, younger than me, still wanted to lie in and turn in early. The cracks were starting to show.

A large silver Mercedes pulled up in front of us. A large gentleman in a smart, expensive looking suit, and an open-necked, crisp white shirt and dark glasses got out of the driver's door. "Charles? Hi, I'm Bill. Nice to meet you. I can see the Reading & Marks similarities. It's been a long time since I saw those in the flesh. Welcome to Australia."

Meeting a relative whom you'd only heard of just a few months prior seemed like quite a daunting experience. Meeting strangers along the coast of South Africa had seemed a lot less scary, maybe because of the anonymity or their lack of expectation of who I'd turn out to be. Whatever the reason, spending time with some of the poorest people on the planet, experiencing life through their eyes, had felt easy compared to this.

"I want to take you on a tour of Perth before I take you back to mine for dinner," he explained. "It's been over 20 years since I left Dad's butchery business and emigrated here. Since then, I have created a market-leading estate agency business. You see that amazing castle overlooking the sca there? We sold that. You see this incredible mansion overlooking Cottesloe Beach? We sold that too. Every morning I wake up early, and I park up here. I swim along Cottesloe Beach, and then me and a few other successful business owners have breakfast in Beaches. I then head into the office."

Wow, I thought, *what a cool start to the working day.*

At his house that evening, I was awestruck with the eclectic worldwide artefacts that adorned the walls. Carvings from Indonesia, paintings from Southeast Asia and loads of Australian art. I wondered how he'd amassed such an extensive collection. "Charles," he said while sipping a large glass of red wine over dinner, "I always take a minimum of three months a year off. Generally, I travel around Australia, as there is so much to do here. I love diving, and I love exploring the amazing nature we have, but I also love to travel the world too. I work smart, so I don't have to work hard."

"Work smart so I don't have to work hard." Now, that was an interesting saying. This was a very different side to running a business than I had seen on the farm, where it was all about working harder than the guy next door. How could it be possible for him to have three months off each year, and have more money than he seemed to know what to do with? Is that even allowed? I was inspired. I wanted to be a businessman like Uncle Bill. I didn't know anything about what he did, but I knew I wanted the independence he had and to lead the same exciting life. For the first time, I realized the benefit of running your own business. It had been under my nose my entire life, but I had not seen it for what it really was. It was an opportunity to craft your own future, but there were different ways you could achieve this, and Uncle Bill seemed to have it pretty good. But how could I possibly do what Uncle Bill had done? He had it all. But I had no idea of what I wanted to do or where to start.

Fast forward to September 1999. I am in Russell Square House in Central London. It's a huge open-plan office, packed full of desks, each one housing nothing but a solitary phone. The office was tired looking, and the smell of burnt coffee and stale cigarette smoke filled the air. This wasn't a calm office; it was more like a scene from *The Wolf of Wall Street*. Over 50 men in pinstriped suits and white shirts dotted the open-plan floor, phones glued to their ears, with stretched cords tethering them to their respective desks. They strutted in circles, for as far as the phone cords permitted, squawking down the line, like frustrated battery hens.

I followed a huge, imposing bald guy, who had introduced himself as Justin, through the path between the desks. The pinstriped sea was only broken by my green sports jacket and my hideous multicoloured tie.

Justin sat me down, in a seat half the size of his. He looked down over me and boomed, "There are two types of people in this world: 'People A' and 'People B.' People A go and work for a big company. They get to earn a good salary. They give all their hard work for their employer, and when they are old, and if they are lucky, they leave with a carriage clock. Then there are People B. They usually earn less than their friends to start with. They often have to work harder, to start with. But because People B are self-employed, over time they earn more than People A, and as well as that, they control their time, and they build up a business they can sell. Which one are you?"

This is easy, I thought. The words of Uncle Bill and Dad ringing in my ears, I confidently said, "I am definitely in People B. I want to control my own destiny and to make the money I deserve."

"In that case, Charlie, you are in. It's commission only. We'll give you one week of financial advice training and one week of sales training. After that, we'll get you to call your family, mates and complete strangers; cold calling if you must, and we'll show you how to sell them pensions and life insurance. You're not independent. You are selling one company's products that aren't even that good, but don't worry about that, because we'll show you how to sell them anyway. You'll struggle like crazy, and 95% of people quit within a couple of months, but if you do make money at it, there might well be a good business in it for you."

OK, that wasn't what he actually said, but that was probably what he should have said, because that's what it was.

So, I fell into financial services by mistake, and it turned out I was quite good at it. I found that I loved helping people save for their futures, protect their families, and make the most of the money they earned. What I didn't like was the commission-hungry, product-pushing, target-focused companies that seemed to fill the industry. I had found a job I loved, but an industry I hated, so I constantly tried to find ways to do it better. One thing that was working, though, was the concept of being self-employed. Reaping what you sow, and directly benefiting from the successes I created sat perfectly with me. I loved that concept and wouldn't have had it any other way. So much so that, while trying to find a less commission-focused business, I did go to an interview for a traditional employed adviser role. I could not get over the concept of having to be in the office, regardless of whether I had hit my target or not, and there was a mutual agreement that I would not suit being an employee. I needed to be my own boss.

But just as the clouds were clearing for my career, I received some devastating news from Australia. Uncle Bill, the man who had it so right in my eyes, had taken his own life. How could this happen? I thought he had the perfect life, so why would he do that? Clearly there was more to life than just success, but I still wasn't sure what it was.

———————

It's some years later now – to be specific, a Sunday night in April 2011 – and I was standing in the Excel Arena in London. It was a huge room. It was dark, and I was surrounded by 6,000 people. People were screaming, yelling and crying out in pain and anger. The sounds were as painful as they were deafening and, to make it worse, as someone who very rarely cries, there were tears pouring down my face. I was not in the middle of some national disaster, though; I am actually at an event called 'Unleash the Power Within,' by a guy called Tony Robbins.

Tony Robbins is the world's top life and performance coach. He has taken top sports stars like Andre Agassi back to number one, has coached several of the world's most successful traders, and has also mentored a number of American Presidents, including Bill Clinton. He charges £1 million per day for one-to-one coaching, but he is most famous for his transformation events, and this is what I and 6,000 other people were attending. Unleash the Power Within is a four-day event that typically runs from 9am until gone midnight each day. You may be wondering, how can a seminar last that long? Well, this is no normal seminar; this is more like a rock concert where the music is the sound of people literally rewriting their past and future lives.

Unleash the Power Within is most famous for 'The Firewalk.' This isn't something you build up to over the four days but is actually done on the very first night. Caryl, my wife, and I headed out into the darkness of the London night around 10.30 on that first evening and down in the car park ahead of us were 35 lanes of burning hot coals, and 6,000 people chanting in order to get themselves in the right state of mind so that they didn't burn their feet. And if you can achieve that, you can achieve anything.

But it wasn't The Firewalk that changed my life that weekend. It was in among the screaming, shouting and crying on the Sunday night that I had an epiphany, in what is known as The Dickens Process. Out of the darkness came a booming voice, as formidable as a lion's roar. I say that because Tony is a big guy. Some call him the 'King of the Coaching Jungle.' At 6 feet 7 inches tall, he has hands seemingly bigger than tennis rackets, and teeth bigger than dinner plates. He is an intimidating guy at the best of times, but what he said in that moment shook me to the core.

With our eyes closed, he asked us: "What decisions have you been making over the last five years that have led you to where you are today? What limiting beliefs do you have that are damaging your life today? What will your life look like five, ten and even 20 years from now if you carry on making these decisions? Because it's in our moments of decision that our destiny is shaped."

I thought to myself, "Five years ago I decided to set up my own financial planning company, Efficient Portfolio, because I was sick of our industry. That has gone really well from a business point of view, but at what cost? Am I really making a sufficient sum to justify the hours I am putting in? One year ago, I set up The Rural Business Community, my serviced office business. That has also been really successful, but I have had to give up huge amounts of my family time. I now have a wife and two beautiful daughters, Ffion and Bronwyn, and I am not spending anywhere near enough time with them. I am slogging my guts out to run these businesses successfully, and while they are doing well, they could be more profitable.

"And look at yourself, Charlie. You are in the worst condition of your life. You must be three stone overweight. You're eating the wrong stuff, drinking too much and you've had to give up playing sport because you are too busy. You are an embarrassment."

So, when Tony said to imagine the worst that your life could look like 20 years from now, because of these decisions, that was easy. I could see a sweaty, wrinkly me in a grotty one-bedroom flat. I weighed 20 stones, my gut was hanging over the side of the chair, pizza boxes surrounded me on the floor. Caryl and the girls had left me years before because I was a disgrace, and my businesses had failed because I was in no fit state to run anything. I couldn't do any of the things I loved, because I was in no physical condition to do them, and I couldn't spend time with the people I loved because they had long since given up on me. This horror of a life was mine, 20 years from now, unless I made some changes now.

Then Tony said something that still plays on repeat in my mind. "If you make the same decisions today as you made yesterday, you'll get the same results tomorrow as you got today." Can you relate to that? What decisions are you making today but expecting a different result from?

I left Unleash the Power Within with a level of determination I had never had before. In the years leading up to Tony Robbins' event, I'd participated in various workshops, but I'd only been working on the business and never anything else. Despite some respite during family holidays, my working days were ridiculous and prohibited me from exercising and spending time with the people I loved. I needed to find ways to work smarter, not harder, just like Uncle Bill had.

I set off with a new purpose and a determination to learn and grow into the best person I could be. I made some immediate changes to the way I worked. I signed up for Tony Robbins' Business Mastery, another four-day event focusing purely on your business and attended events such as T. Harv Eker's Guerrilla Business Intensive and Enlightened Warrior Training Camp. I also read more than ever. More importantly, Caryl and I redesigned from scratch the way we ate, and also how we scheduled our time to ensure we factored in quality family time and exercise.

Fast forward again to September 2015. I am three stone lighter than before I made that initial encounter with Tony Robbins, and in recent years have completed numerous 100-mile-plus bike rides for charity, including 'The Dragon Ride,' which is a day of cycling 142 miles through the Welsh Mountains. I am also now competing in triathlons, and recently completed my first Ironman in Cervia, Italy, a 2.4 mile swim, 112 mile bike ride finished off with a 26.2 mile run.

In addition to that, five years ago I stopped working Friday afternoons, almost never work weekends or evenings, and have around 12 weeks of holiday a year. During this time, I do not work, don't check emails or even contact the office. I leave my team to run the company for me.

There is nothing special about me. All I have done is gone out and found others who have already mastered the elements I want to master and have learned from them. I have read their books, attended their courses, and spent quality mentoring time with them. I am not saying I have it designed perfectly, but at 42 years old, I have designed a pretty extraordinary life, and I have no doubt that the next year will be even better than this one.

And do you know what? The less I work, the more money I seem to make. The happier and healthier I am, the better I am at doing what I do best. I hope you can see that I have created the perfect blend of profitability, free time and fun in my businesses and life. You will not achieve the same as I have done solely by reading this book; however, you may achieve the same or even better than I have if you read the book and continue to carry on the practices I'll talk you through. So, let's get started.

CHAPTER SUMMARY

- As a farmer's son, I realized soon after finishing university that I needed to do something different with my life.

- On my travels, Uncle Bill inspired me because he ran a highly successful business, but also took three months off every year.

- When successfully running my own company a few years later, I realized I had got it all wrong when at Tony Robbin's firewalking event. I was working too many hours, was in the worst shape of my life and wasn't seeing my children grow up.

- Over the years since, I have read every book and attended every course that I felt could help me change this.

- Nowadays, I take three months of the year off with my family, I recently completed an Ironman and my business continues to go from strength to strength, all because I identified the secrets behind entrepreneurial happiness.

CHAPTER 3

BEST FRIEND
FOREVER

I have had around 20 years of experience being self-employed, and I have discovered that if you are truly going to create entrepreneurial happiness, you need to master three main areas.

First, you need ensure you are making **money**. If you aren't doing that, then business life is definitely stressful. You cannot afford to pay yourself what you deserve; you cannot afford to enjoy the holidays that allow you to recharge; you cannot afford to invest in new systems, marketing opportunities or new people; and, ultimately, you cannot grow your business. So, it is a given, you need to make money.

Poor cash flow is the killer of so many small businesses. Lack of investment can kill business growth and prohibits it from reaching its potential. In the early stages of business, income generation can also be slow, and life can be very 'hand to mouth,' so we need to find ways to make money, and quickly. It would be easier if you had a management team taking care of all of these complicated details, but you don't, so what can you do?

If you want to make more money, you need more leads, more client enquiries and more buy-ins, but that is easier said than done. How can you consistently find more of your best-fit clients and make sure that they are desperate to work with you? If you can crack this nut, you can have a far better nourished business, as you have a consistent stream of new money coming in. Again, it is easier said than done.

Making more money creates more problems. What should you do with it, how do you track it, and how can you see what your business and personal financial future looks like? You need to be able to predict what is coming if you are to keep your company's finances, and your own wealth, growing rather than shrinking.

In order to create entrepreneurial happiness, we need to find more robust ways to build, manage and protect our money.

But entrepreneurial happiness is about so much more than just money. You also need to be the master of your **time**. Only once you have cracked this can you work in/on your business on your terms and enjoy all of the other things that are important to you. Without this, you will be working late, missing your children's sport's days and not creating memories with the people you love. Without time, you may also neglect your health, and to run a healthy business, you need to be a healthy business owner.

But where do you find time? There's a saying that goes, "If you want something done, ask a busy person." How can that make sense? Do they have more than 24 hours in their day? No, they just have a better understanding of how to manage their time and to get the most out of it. Are you making the most of your time? Could you be achieving so much more with the help of better strategies and tools? What are you missing out on by not having these in place?

It's difficult running your own business. Your clients want your time, but so do your employees. It's often a misconception that your employees won't be able to do the job as well as you can. In reality, they are more than capable, but they can't if so much of what you need them to do is in your head.

Maybe you are also struggling with finding enough time because your business is built around dealing with people on a one-to-one basis, and this massively restricts the amount of work you can take on. There are only so many hours in the day, and therefore only so many clients you can deal with.

Finally, if you don't have enough time, and you are spinning too many plates, which one is the one that gets dropped first? It's usually your health. If you get busy, you stop exercising. You also maybe eat less healthy, and perhaps even drink a little more to de-stress. An unhealthy business owner leads to an unhealthy business, too. A lack of energy, self-discipline and longevity can't be good for any business, and there is only so long that coffee and energy drinks will keep you bouncing back.

If you want to create entrepreneurial happiness, you need to master making **money** and controlling your **time**, but there is one last piece of the jigsaw to be truly happy: if you want to create true Entrepreneurial Happiness, you need to create **fun** in your business life. Without fun in your business, every day seems like a chore.

It's so easy to start to feel unfulfilled if you think you are not moving forwards in your life or not getting better as a person. Entrepreneur and motivational speaker Jim Rohn said, "Income seldom exceeds personal development." In fact, it's one of our six human needs, and you won't feel truly happy without it. And it's not just about growing as a person, but as a business, too. If you are not going forwards, you are going backwards. If you are not continually innovating, then you will be overtaken by your competition, and at a pace where it will be too late to adapt. Your business will have gone in a flash.

Did you know that most of the astronauts who walked on the moon suffered from depression afterwards? Why would that be, when they had achieved their lifelong goals? Shouldn't they have been overjoyed? Sadly, achieving their goals was the reason they became depressed. Once you have fulfilled a massive goal, there is nothing to compel you forwards, no new purpose to live for, and this can lead to serious unhappiness. You need a compelling future to pull you forwards, and without one, business life will become pretty depressing.

One of the best ways to scale your business is to employ others, but that can feel like a chore in itself. You train your employees to where you need them to be, and then they leave! They don't believe in the business like you do and don't share your vision. After all, it's just their job, not their life like it is for you.

There are so many aspects that can drag the fun out of your business life. As the saying goes, "If you do a job you love, you'll never work a day in your life." But does that still apply when you spend most of your time doing stuff you hate? You need to create fun in your business so that you live out your passion every day.

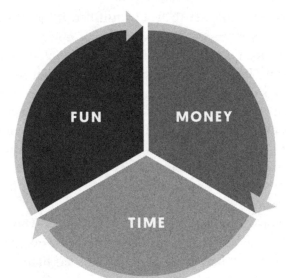

I have discovered that there are a number of key areas that you need to focus on in order to create success in each of these areas. In order to make this more memorable and easier to explain, I have taken the time to build these into systems, so that hopefully they make more sense. The **Better Future Framework** is a system that I believe has the power to transform your business and personal life forever. Its components certainly have for me.

The Better Future Framework is made of three key systems.

MORE MONEY

In order to help you make your business more profitable and generate more money, I have created **The Profitable Business P.L.A.N.** If you learn and follow the four key steps here, you will have the tools to be able to attract more new customers into your business to ensure that you can make more money. Often the biggest constraint to increasing profits is finding enough of the right customers, so I want to show you how you can find a lot more. The Profitable Business P.L.A.N. will show you how to know exactly what is going on in the business at any one time, so that you understand exactly which elements are working well for you and which need more attention. An early warning system, if you like, to help you avoid running out of cash or customers; it's also the tool that ensures you hit the targets you set yourself.

The Profitable Business P.L.A.N. will also show you how to protect your business in case the unexpected happens. We can all plan for a predictable future, but you need to ensure that when the unexpected comes along, it doesn't derail your plan. And it will show how you can maximize the money you make, keeping as much away from the tax man as legally and ethically as possible and protecting the money you make in case your business suffers a change of fate in the future. This system will equip you with the tools to help make sure you generate more money and make the most of it when you do.

The concepts inside The Profitable Business P.L.A.N. have allowed me to grow my new business level by a whopping 50% in five of the last six years. They have allowed us to increase our new enquiries by a multiple of seven in just four years. They have also given me much greater insight into what is going well and what isn't in our business, so that I can anticipate problems on the road ahead. They have also allowed me to de-risk my business, so that if something unexpected happens, there is less risk of it going under.

The Profitable Business P.L.A.N. helps you to make more money, more effectively, and with more predictability than ever before. In case you are curious, P.L.A.N. stands for Partnerships, Leads, Amass, Numbers.

MORE TIME

In order to help you take control of your time, I have created **The Free Life Business M.O.D.E.L.**, a five-step system that will show you how you can scale your business with decreasing input from you, so that you can take more time away. It will show you how you can streamline and delegate, so that you only concentrate on the elements of the business where you excel.

The Free Life Business M.O.D.E.L. shows you how you can maximize the impact of what you do, so that you can achieve more in less time. It will give you the systems that will allow you to get the most done possible in your time, and make sure you have the time to do all the other important things you cannot currently do. Finally, The Free Life Business M.O.D.E.L. will show you how to improve your health and wellbeing once you have more free time.

The Free Life Business M.O.D.E.L. has allowed me to take more and more time out of the business while simultaneously running it more effectively and making more profit than ever before. In reality, I could take more time out if I wanted to, but actually I now enjoy the balance I have. This has allowed me to get into the best shape of my life and to spend lots of amazing holiday time with my family.

Yet, despite me spending less time in my office, my business is helping more people and making more money than ever before, and it is thanks to the tools and strategies that I have rolled into The Free Life Business M.O.D.E.L. As this book will reveal, M.O.D.E.L stands for Magnify, Operations, Delegate, Energy and Life.

MORE FUN

In order to help you enjoy your business life more, I have created **The E.P.I.C. Business Blueprint**. This four-step system will help you ensure you become the best possible version of yourself. It will give you what I believe is the best way to set and consistently hit clear and exciting goals.

The E.P.I.C. Business Blueprint will give you the tools to build an incredible team around you that you love working with, and that live and breathe your vision for the business. It also helps you identify other firms that you can partner with, so that you can both achieve your goals more quickly.

The E.P.I.C. Business Blueprint has allowed Efficient Portfolio to become one of the best financial planning businesses in the UK. The tools, strategies and systems are the reason behind our continued and strong business growth; however, one element alone is the main factor behind what allowed us to increase our business by 50% in the first year we tried it. It is incredible and will be covered later on.

As Efficient Portfolio continues to grow, I have also grown a phenomenal amount as a result of the content I put into The E.P.I.C. Business Blueprint. I am a very different person than who I was ten years ago. A far more focused, determined, organized and efficient version of the person who set up Efficient Portfolio in 2006.

Without question, I have the best team at Efficient Portfolio I have ever had. They are far better at their own areas of expertise than I am, and we gel brilliantly as a team, partly because we all buy into the same purpose. They allow me to do what I do best and take care of all of the other aspects of the business, which means I love what I do.

I am a very goal-focused person, and I love the fact that I am consistently ticking off my goals. Thanks to The E.P.I.C. Business Blueprint, there is always a more compelling future for me to strive towards. It is also this system that shelters me from a world of negativity and keeps me feeling positive about the future. As you can probably tell, I love my life, and I want to share with you the secrets to how I got there, so that you can too. E.P.I.C. in this model stands for End Game, Plan, Innovate and Culture.

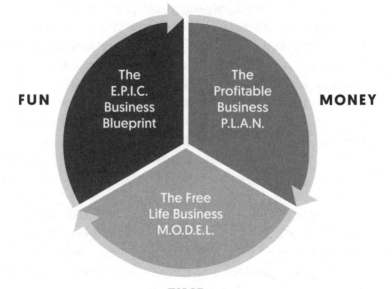

THE BETTER FUTURE FRAMEWORK (BFF)

In a nutshell, if you grasp the concepts within the BFF System, you will be well on your way to finding entrepreneurial happiness. That magic balance of making enough money to live the life you want, having sufficient free time to do the things you love, and thriving and having fun at work.

CHAPTER SUMMARY

- If you don't learn how to find more customers and, ultimately, make more money from the work you do, you will be deprived of living the life you deserve.

- If you don't learn how to improve your time management, then you will miss out on living a long and healthy life with the people you care about the most.

- If you don't learn how to create fun in your work life, you will end up spending the majority of your life doing something you don't actually enjoy.

- The easiest way to create more money, free time and fun in your business is to follow a proven system. That system is The Better Future Framework because if you follow its principals, it will be your best friend forever.

THE PROFITABLE BUSINESS P.L.A.N.

THE FOUR-STEP GUIDE TO MAKING MORE MONEY IN YOUR BUSINESS.

P   Partnerships

L   Leads

A   Amass

N   Numbers

CHAPTER 4

'LEADS' LEAD TO MORE MONEY

"Bremont is an award-winning British company producing beautifully engineered chronometers at our headquarters in Henley on Thames, England."

That's what Bremont's website says. It continues with:

"Life for Nick and Giles English changed significantly one clear day in March 1995. Nick was practising for an air display with their father Euan. But the 1942 WWII Harvard aircraft they were flying was involved in an accident. Giles, waiting to take off for the next sortie, was told that his father had been killed. His brother had broken over 30 bones and probably wouldn't make it.

"Six months later, however, Nick was back in the air and being flown by Giles. But things would never be the same again. Life was too short to waste. The two brothers decided to pursue what they enjoyed most: a life crafting beautifully engineered mechanical devices.

"When they weren't flying old aircraft, Nick and Giles had spent most of their childhood making things in the workshop of their gifted father an ex-RAF pilot with a PhD in Aeronautical Engineering. Models. Restored cars. They even helped him build an aircraft they still fly to this day. Euan was also passionate about mechanical timepieces. He would often bring home an old clock from an auction for the brothers to try and get going again. The passion lives on in the classic curve of a Bremont timepiece."

An incredibly moving story, but what's this got to do with making more money? Simon Sinek, in his brilliant book *Start with Why*, highlights the merit of beginning every client meeting with why you do what you do. Whether it is your marketing, your recruitment, or improving your teamwork, one of the most powerful aspects to promoting and improving your business is to ensure everyone, including yourself, knows why you do what you do. And this is what Bremont has done.

Bremont is probably the most successful non-Swiss company in the high-end watch sector. They have had huge success since launching, and a large reason behind that is their story. And not just their initial story; every watch has its very own story. For example, the Bremont MB1 was only sold to people who had ejected out of a plane using a Martin Baker ejector seat. Now that's a niche market. But that watch has sold second-hand on eBay for $120,000, so they have certainly created demand. Why are people willing to spend this sort of money on a watch? Because it looks nice or because of the story behind it?

How can you build the same hype and success around your brand or service? The first step, of course, is that you need to know your own story. Why do you do what you do?

For instance, if you want to boost the effectiveness of every piece of marketing you do, you always need to think back to 'start with why' because people buy into why you are doing what you do and, as a result, they buy into you as a business and as an individual much more. I would recommend that you write a single sentence and use it at any available opportunity.

Once you've got this succinct why statement, I would then suggest that you build a paragraph about 'Your Why' and, ideally, a full story, too. To help you Find Your Why, I have put together an exercise. This can be found in *The Entrepreneurial Happiness Workbook*, which you can download for free from www.charliereading.com/EH.

READING MINDS

I am a big believer in setting goals because I achieve so much more as a result. After I employed my first team member, I decided I needed help in the way I was going to grow and manage my business. I had heard about a workshop for entrepreneurs called The Strategic Coach® Program through some of the top people in the financial services sector and decided that if I was going to get close to what they were doing, I needed to learn the same tools and strategies.

The Strategic Coach Program seemed like a huge commitment and cost at the time, but I knew if I was going to be successful, I needed to hang on and learn from the best our industry had to offer. The programme, founded by Dan Sullivan, is a quarterly workshop where a group of entrepreneurs meet to learn new strategies on how they can improve the way they run their lives and their businesses.

There was a minimum earning level to be able to join the programme and I remember when I first saw Dan speak, I was below that level. I decided that when I was above it, I could afford to employ someone to help me and, at that point, I would need help creating a better business that was no longer just in my head. A couple of years later, I made what felt like a huge leap of faith. Particularly where learning is involved, it can feel so expensive, and you question whether it will pay for itself, let alone deliver everything it promises.

What I loved about the Strategic Coach Program was that it forced you to spend one day a quarter working on the business, as opposed to working within it. It was an amazing opportunity to be a small fish in a big pond, and when I was bouncing ideas off people about changes I needed to make in my business, it was usually with people who had long since made those changes themselves. This programme is not industry-specific, it works for all business owners, but I do think it works particularly well for people in professional practice.

One of the things that Dan Sullivan is most famous for is his 'R-Factor Question.'[1] As a result, before we go any further, I would like to ask you my version; it isn't quite the same as Dan's, but it will achieve the same result.

If we were sat here one year from now, what must have happened for you to be happy with the progress you have made?

What concerns do you have that you'd like to overcome, and what opportunities do you have that you would like to maximize?

Take some time to answer this question and write down your answers.

What you should now have are some clear goals that you need to achieve over the next year. You should have identified some concerns in both your work and personal life that you need to resolve, and some opportunities that you need to have maximized in that time, too. If you do not write down your goals regularly already, make this a new habit. I'll come back to this later and give you an amazing system that will ensure that you hit these goals, but the first step to achieving anything is to first define where you need to be.

At Harvard University, a study was conducted to see what percentage of graduates documented their goals. The results showed that only 3% of graduates did this, and that the 3% who had been regularly writing down their goals were worth more than the 97% combined.

Think of writing down goals like a game of bowling. If I asked you to get a strike, knocking all ten pins down with one ball, while you were looking at and aiming at the pins, you'd have a fighting chance. You'd probably not get a strike every time, but hopefully almost every attempt would take out some pins. But what if I asked you to try while wearing a blindfold? You've just seriously hampered your chances of scoring a strike, and maybe even bowling in the right lane. The message here is simple: if you can't see where you're going, you have very little chance of reaching your destination. Writing down your goals is a good way to plot out your route, especially when used in conjunction with my system. If we're sticking with the bowling metaphor, the system I've created has the same effect as using the barriers that stop the ball dropping into the gutter.

For now, I want you to focus on the fact that you have identified some 'worries' that you want to eliminate over the next year, and some 'opportunities' that you want to maximize. I would imagine that if you achieve all of them, that would mean this year has been a good year. If that isn't the case, go back and rethink on a bigger scale. What would make you truly proud of what you'd achieved?

Your goals are not the only ones to consider. To illustrate my point, I'm going to sell you a widget. This widget is called the Future Transformer. My Future Transformer widget is guaranteed to deliver all the items you listed above. Whatever you want, the Future Transformer is *guaranteed* to deliver it. My question is, would you like to buy my Future Transformer widget? Of course you do. It guarantees to deliver the most important things over the next year. The question is, how much would you be willing to pay? £1,000? £100,000? £1 million? I suppose it depends on the size of your dreams.

This is evidently a fictional product, but if I did have a 'magical widget' that promised to deliver you the most important things over the next 12 months, the chances are you'd buy it. So, would it not make logical sense to know the answer to the former question for your own customers and clients? Wouldn't it be much easier to sell your product or service to that new customer or client if you understood what their most important goals were for the year ahead, so that you could show them how your product or service could help get them there?

Let me give you an example. I recently read *Leading* by Sir Alex Ferguson and Michael Moritz. In it, Sir Alex tells the story of him trying to sign Paul 'Gazza' Gascoigne for Manchester United. Playing for his hometown club, Newcastle United at the time, Gazza was the young rising star in English football, and Sir Alex wanted him at Manchester United. So, he went into his meeting with Gazza with a well-oiled and polished sales pitch to win him over.

Sir Alex's opening gambit was to build some rapport with Gazza: first, he regaled him with the success stories of fellow

Geordies who had played for Manchester United; he then told Gazza that he would be walking in the steps of his hero, Bobby Charlton; and finally he focused on the wonderful history of the top players at Manchester United who went on to become the top players for England. Well versed at signing the players he wanted, Sir Alex was confident that these tales would get him his man.

But do you remember Gazza going on to become a star at Manchester United? Of course you don't, because Gazza never took up Sir Alex's deal. Instead of being lured by Sir Alex, Gazza signed for Tottenham Hotspur instead. What could Spurs have offered him that Sir Alex couldn't? It turns out it was a house in Gateshead for his mum! Had Sir Alex Ferguson asked what was most important to Gazza before he went steamrolling into his pitch, do you think that Gazza may have signed for Sir Alex instead? Given the size of the club at the time, I reckon if a house in Gateshead was what Gazza wanted, that's what he would have got, and perhaps his and England's footballing history would have been very different.

Whether you're sending out marketing letters or you are face to face with a client in a sales meeting, you need to make your content meaningful to that person. Furthermore, it's all very well generating more leads with your marketing strategy, but if you want to convert more of those leads, you need to be able to help your clients in the most impactful way possible. If you want to truly show your clients how your product or service can help them deliver their most important goals, you first need to ask what they are. Ask all of your potential clients this question and the insights you will get will help you transform your business into the one of your client's dreams.

Furthermore, over time you will notice patterns and common goals among your best-fit clients. This will allow you to tailor everything you do towards these. That means when you do your marketing, you will already be appealing to your best-fit client's core goals, without even knowing it for sure yet. By doing this, your marketing becomes a whole lot more powerful and generates more leads.

Be meaningful, be personal, get more leads and help more people.

REFERRALS ARE THE KEY

If you want to receive, first you must give. That is the rule, not just of business, but of life, too. In his monumental book *Influence*, Dr Robert Cialdini talks about how a university professor sent Christmas cards to a group of complete strangers. He received replies from a good number of these people. They had never heard of or met this professor but, having received a card, they felt compelled to send one in reply. When someone does something for us, we feel compelled to return the gesture.

In the same book, Dr Cialdini goes on to tell a story of Ethiopia and Mexico, and a $5,000 relief aid payment. In 1985, Ethiopia was in the heart of devastating poverty. Its food supply had been ravished, its economy in ruins and its people suffering as a result of an unrelenting drought and disease. To hear of a relief payment of $5,000 sent from Mexico to Ethiopia should not sound that unexpected. However, that relief payment didn't go from Mexico to Ethiopia; it actually went from Ethiopia to Mexico. The money had been sent to help out with the devastation caused by an earthquake in Mexico City.

To understand this better, we need to look back to 1935, when Mexico had sent aid to Ethiopia when it was invaded by Italy. Despite the incredible need for the money in their homeland of the drought-stricken Ethiopia, the need to reciprocate and pay back the debt had remained for a half century.

The power of reciprocity seems to know no bounds; so if you want to receive more referrals, you first need to think about how you can give. How can you create so much value and good feeling that the recipients of your gift are delighted to work with you?

If you want to find more clients, there is a huge resource that can help you: your existing clients! By their very nature, your clients have already bought into what you do. They want to see you do well and they want to help you do that, because that makes sure that you are there to continue helping them in the future. So, why is it that some businesses get loads of referrals and others none? The answer boils down to how businesses deal with the following questions:

1. How often do you make your clients think about referring someone to you?
2. How easy do you make it to refer someone?
3. How do clients benefit when they do refer someone?
4. How does the referral benefit the person being referred?

Nobody wants to be pestered with being asked for referrals. Even worse, nobody wants to feel like they are pestering people for referrals. When I first joined the dark, sales-driven world of financial services, at the end of the second meeting with a client I was told to ask the newly signed up client for some referrals. I was told to say that it is how we keep their costs down, because it saved on marketing. I would sit there and write the numbers one through to six on a blank piece of paper, and then go silent. The awkwardness for both of us was awful.

The clients didn't want to feel pressured into giving referrals, and I didn't want to pressure them, yet it happened across every desk in the office because that was what we were told we had to do. I still cringe thinking back to those moments. No one wants to be on either side of that conversation, so how can you get more referrals without having those awkward encounters?

Over time, I have learned to ask more gently, more often, and to build a process around it. Last year we got 40 referrals from our clients. That may not sound like a lot for your business, but I can only put it into context by telling you about the year before when we received 21 client referrals. Forty is nearly double the previous year. The year before that it was eight. Again, we doubled the referrals we were getting. The question is, how did we manage to achieve that?

One of the ways is by hosting our annual Referral Dinner. This is a meal to thank anyone who has referred us to a new client. It is usually at a Michelin-star restaurant and is a lovely evening. The purpose is to thank those who are keen referees, and to share some quality time and a great experience with them.

What reward is appropriate is for you to decide. A client is of high value to us, so a Michelin-star dinner is right for our business. I know of one company that takes referred clients on a cruise for a couple of days. If a client's worth justifies the cost, then go for it. Personally, I would shy away from giving money, but a voucher or some flowers could be a cost-effective solution. Ideally, though, make it an interactive experience, and a dinner works well.

But what about the client who has been referred? We give any referrals into our business a free Exploration Meeting with one of our advisers, worth £197. If you can do something similar, do it, but make sure you tell them why they are getting the benefit and the value of it. In my experience, people don't value things they get for free. They only value it when they understand what the cost should have been. In addition to the meeting, we also give a discount on their plan – a document we use to really help them see what they need to do to create the future of their dreams.

You may be thinking, "I cannot afford to give some people a discounted fee or product." If that's the case, you probably aren't charging enough in the first place. Even if you have to put your prices up to offset this discount to referrals, do it. These people are warmer, better clients than cold clients. They are less likely to mess you around, and they are more likely to become long-term clients, so they deserve a discount.

In addition to asking for referrals, you need to make it part of your process, as otherwise it will get forgotten. We ask for introductions at the end of the second meeting, because that is the time when clients most buy into what we do. But it doesn't end there. We send a sequence of letters after a client signs up, and one of these specifically addresses the opportunity to introduce people to us, reminding clients that they also stand to benefit with a lovely dinner as a thank you. This acts as another opportunity for them to remember our request for an introduction. If that's not enough, we also call a new client a couple of weeks after this meeting to check that their implementation is going smoothly and to see if they have any questions. As well as being a great thing to do for the client relationship, this is another great opportunity to remind them about introducing you to people they know.

What can you do in your business to allow you to get more referrals out of your existing customers? In my Better Future coaching, I get people to do an exercise to help them work on how they can generate more referrals in their business. You can find out more about this at www.charliereading.com/BF.

BECOME THE EXPERT

When I was travelling around the world, I played a lot of pool. As a kid, I loved playing snooker, occasionally heading to a snooker club with my dad and Uncle John. The smoky, dark and dingy atmosphere was like stepping into another world as a young man, even if I could only just about reach the full-size snooker table.

The love of playing pool then naturally migrated into pool in the pub when my school friends and I were old enough, or we snuck in underage. There is something quite beautiful in spending time playing pool with friends with a pint in your hand.

As a result of this misspent youth, I was pretty handy around a pool table. Pool served a great purpose when I was travelling on my own. It was my ticket to meet new people easily. When I was in Queenstown, New Zealand, with Chris, my best mate from school, and later my best man, we carried on that principle. Chris and I had played a lot of pool together over the years, so most evenings during our trip, we squeezed some pool in somewhere, but in New Zealand, they play to different rules. As you may know, in the UK, you generally get two shots if your opponent commits a foul. This is sufficient penalty to not foul on purpose, because two shots can allow a reasonable pool player to clear the table and not allow you back into the game. This is not the case in New Zealand.

In New Zealand, they do not give two shots in the event of a foul; instead, they have a rule that prohibits deliberate fouls. This sounds logical; however, given it is a question of someone's word, it is not always clear. Whether someone has played a foul shot intentionally or not is of course open to interpretation, and I was about to find that out.

Chris and I were drinking in Harry's Bar in Queenstown one evening and saw that there was a pool competition. "That sounds like fun," we thought. A good way to meet a few of the locals and spice up the evening. We certainly got both. Chris got knocked out fairly early, but I made my way through to the final, so I was eager to find out who I was up against. I headed over to chat to the organizer of the competition to find out who I'd be playing against. Clad in baggy trousers and sporting dreadlocked hair, I was slightly concerned by his response. In a strong Kiwi accent, he said, "Dude, you'll be playing The Chief."

I headed over to the pool table where my battle with 'The Chief' was to take place. I was confronted by this huge 6 foot, 4 inch Maori man machine, wearing a sleeveless shirt to show off rippling muscles and tattoos. With his long hair and stone-cold face, he wouldn't have looked out of place in an All Blacks shirt performing the Haka in front of the quivering opponents expecting their next pummelling. This wasn't someone you wanted to mess with, and his name – The Chief – couldn't have been a more fitting description of him.

I actually got off to a pretty strong start in the game, despite the added nerves of it being a.) a final and b.) against The Chief. I potted several balls with my first visit to the table and was in a good position, but it was all about to change. The Chief had other ideas. Two deliberate fouls in quick succession, and suddenly my back was against the wall. Chris, my wingman, grabbed me and insisted I challenge him on these. After all, they were not in the spirit of the NZ game, and potentially, it should now be my game. But that involved confrontation. I had to call him on a deliberate foul, and that was clearly going to spark unrest. It was very easy for Chris to encourage my outburst, but he was not going to be on the other end of The Chief's wrath.

Despite my pride telling me to speak up and challenge The Chief, the self-preservation genes in my body were ensuring that my lips stayed tightly shut. Not just because he was so intimidating but because, as a local, these were his rules, not mine. In the end I lost the game, and the tournament, solely, I believe, because of his underhanded tactics. He walked out of Harry's that evening with the prize money, but at least I walked out without a bleeding nose and a black eye.

Now, you may be wondering why I am telling you about playing pool against The Chief in Queenstown. Am I telling you this story because I want you to learn to speak up more? No. The reason I am telling you is because I want you to become 'The Expert.' The reason I didn't challenge The Chief was because he was The Expert. While I did not want to cross The Chief, had I wanted advice on how to win a pool tournament in NZ, he is exactly the person I would have gone to.

In whatever it is you do, you need to become The Expert too. By becoming The Expert, you will have people seek you out, and they will only want to deal with you. They will be knocking down a path to your door, instead of you having to try to find them. If I wanted to learn how to take the best free kicks in the world, I'd be seeking out David Beckham to teach me, as he is the expert in that field. If I wanted to play fly half for England and to kick them to World Cup glory, I'd be seeking out Jonny Wilkinson's advice. And if I wanted to win Wimbledon, I'd seek advice from Serena Williams. If you can become the expert in your field, then you will have people seek you out to work with you.

There are lots of ways that you can become The Expert in the eyes of your best-fit clients, and what works best for you may be different from the next person. However, there are some obvious routes to this regardless of your expertise.

The first, and in my eyes probably the best, is to become an author. Once I had *The Dream Retirement: How to Secure Your Money and Retire Happy* published in 2015 by Black Card Books, I noticed a massive change in the way people perceived me, with clients respecting my business and the team I had trained much more.

Therefore, if you want to become the expert in your field, one of the best ways you can achieve this is to write your own book. But if writing a book isn't for you, or the time to become an author isn't right, there are other ways to become an expert by producing other content. Write a blog or a newsletter, make videos or podcasts and share the content with people. If people are regularly seeing you write or produce commentary on your specialist field, over time they will start to see you as The Expert.

Another way to become the expert on your subject is to be speaking about it from a stage.

Finally, the other way you can become the expert is to be featured in the media. Whether that be newspapers, radio or TV, being featured will massively raise people's perception of you, and you will rapidly become the expert in their eyes. The problem is that this isn't an easy thing to do. Unless you can identify your very own niche, it is difficult to get through the gatekeepers and, depending on your sector, even paying PR specialists is not always effective, as they need something compelling to work with.

But one of the best ways to get asked to speak on other people's stages, and to be featured in the media, is to write your own book. Not only does this make you the expert in the eyes of your potential clients, it also has the same effect on people in the media. Another great thing about a book is that the content you write for it can also be used in a blog, newsletter and brochures. You could even turn it into other products like podcasts or an audiobook. It allows you to kill several birds with one stone.

To help you, I have created my own book writing exercise for you, so that you too can get those creative juices flowing. This can be found in the workbook on my website: www.charliereading.com/EH. Once done, I always turn this into a mind map that I can build up as I think of things. I find this really helpful to see the book structure and also to identify the best place for things. Quite often moving content around on the mind map allows you to see better where each piece fits. Get creative, become an author and please send me a copy of your new book when you get it.

ATTRACTION MARKETING

If you want to gain more business opportunities, you need to attract them. Traditionally that would have meant paying for an advert in the newspaper, on TV or the radio. While these are still viable options, they are expensive and less effective than they have ever been, but whatever route you go down, you need attraction marketing devices (AMD). An AMD is something you can give away for free, or for a relatively low price, that then directs people into your sales funnel.

I can offer a free download of my book and, in exchange, we will then send them a series of follow-up emails that, while adding value by sharing ways they can improve their money, then ultimately aim to get them contacting Efficient Portfolio for their free financial planning call.

You need to have a number of AMD out there, though. An AMD can be a book, a white paper, a blog, a newsletter or a podcast. Anything you can give away for free to as many people as possible. Once people see the value you are creating, thus build a level of trust with you, you can then ask them to make a slightly bigger step that either involves a little more commitment or a cost.

Your AMDs need to point at your sales process, so you can then use your AMDs in your advertising to draw people in. You are giving them stuff they value for free, and that makes the whole process far more effective. The question is, who are you targeting? Are they the right people? As a result, you need to have a clear picture of the type of people you are trying to attract.

In order that you can identify your best-fit client, I have put together an exercise for you to work through. This can be found in *The Entrepreneurial Happiness Workbook*, which you can download for free from www.charliereading.com/EH.

Think about how you can advertise your business in the modern age. Create your own content that gives amazing value to your best-fit clients and share it through today's marketing channels. It may be that you want to pay to advertise through Facebook, but by sharing engaging content through Facebook or LinkedIn, you can also achieve this for free. Maybe even a combination of the two would work even better. For example, we have helped a number of farming clients that had sold land. I wrote a blog article on this subject, and that is now out there being put in front of other similar people.

THEY ASK, YOU ANSWER

For great marketing, you need to keep one simple principle in mind: allow your customers to ask, and you answer. So, what questions are your customers and clients asking? Whatever they are, you need to be providing them with an answer online. Ideally, but not essentially, in the form of a video or blog. This should be easy enough to achieve; you just need to answer your clients' and prospects' questions.

So, when you are doing any marketing, consider what questions your customers are asking. And use those questions as the titles for your content, as Google, Bing, etc. will love you for making their life easier and, even better, if your web team can make sure your content gets seen through search engine optimization, you'll be amazed at the results.

1.   Please visit www.StrategicCoach.com to learn more about the Strategic Coach Program and/or the R-Factor.

CHAPTER SUMMARY

- Boost the money flow into your business by generating more leads, initially by having an understanding of why you do what you do, and then relaying that to your potential clients.

- Engage with your clients more and help them at a much deeper level by identifying what is important to them in the future, and then helping them achieve that using your expertise.

- Generate more referrals from your existing clients by exceeding expectations and implementing a structured referral process.

- Be seen by your clients and potential clients as The Expert in order to be the only person they would come to for what you do. There are a variety of ways to do this, like blogs, YouTube and social media, but none better than writing your own book.

- You need to identify exactly what your best-fit client looks like and what their common concerns are, so that your marketing targets them with laser like focus.

CHAPTER 5

'PARTNERSHIPS'
WITH PURPOSE

"Talent wins games, but teamwork and intelligence win championships." – Michael Jordan

The legend that is Steve Jobs is synonymous with the global giant that is Apple, but it's not the only household brand that he founded. In 1986, shortly after he was forced out of Apple, Jobs decided to go back to his roots and purchased a small, unknown computer manufacturer called Pixar. Wanting to completely overhaul the company, he relocated the business to an abandoned Del Monte canning factory with the initial aim of creating three build ings with offices for computer scientists, animators and the executives. But Jobs quickly abandoned this plan and decided against this segregation, instead creating one large collaborative space.

For Jobs, creating the space was largely irrelevant. His main aim was to achieve a collaborative culture, where everyone at Pixar could share ideas and inspire others. John Lasseter, the chief creative officer at Pixar, describes the equation this way: "Technology inspires art, and art challenges the technology."

So how did he achieve this? The answer is actually quite simple: Jobs moved the company mailboxes, the meeting rooms, the cafeteria, the coffee bar and the gift shop to the centre of the building, which he called 'The Atrium.'

Brad Bird, the director of *The Incredibles* and *Ratatouille*, said, "The Atrium initially might seem like a waste of space. But Steve realized that when people run into each other, when they make eye contact, things happen."

This move certainly came at the expense of convenience, but Jobs' vision required consilience between all of Pixar's people, so the move was the best way to achieve his goal. Jobs believed that the pinnacle of creativity and productivity can only be achieved when there is a connection between everyone within a company, and I quite agree.

If you are running your business or your own client base, do you ever feel that you are torn between spending time looking for new clients and working on the clients you have? If you constantly focus on the work in hand, you risk not having any new business in the pipeline, and a few months down the line, you will have no work to do. Conversely, if you focus too much of your attention on frantically generating an abundance of new clients, you'll have insufficient time to deal with the client work. As you can see, this is a bit of a dilemma!

Wouldn't it be brilliant if you had a team of people who were always on the lookout for your best-fit client? A team that was meeting lots of other people you don't know, but that knew in detail how you could help them, so that they could be spotting the opportunities for you. Sounds expensive, doesn't it: a bespoke sales team that it always out there finding clients for you and referring them into your business. What if I told you they could be free? Or alternatively, you only paid them when you successfully turned their referrals into clients? Hopefully that sounds even better. This is how we work at Efficient Portfolio, and I want to tell you how.

Most successful people need the help of an accountant, a solicitor and a financial planner at different stages in their lives, as well as perhaps some specialist advisers for their unique situation. Historically, the client sat in the middle being given advice from the different sources. The accountant may be advising them to pay themselves a dividend as they have made good profits. The solicitor is helping them with organizing their estate better, and the financial planner is advising them to fund their pension. The client is getting direction from the individual parties, but no one is looking at the bigger picture, except the client. There is no joined up approach, and they aren't looking at whether one set of advice is conflicting with another because they appear to have different priorities.

In actual fact, there is a common thread running through this advice. If the increased profits are taken out of the business as a pension contribution, the client can save more income tax, but also protect more of their estate from inheritance tax. The client can also leave the organization of their will so that their business shares are left to a business trust, to save further inheritance tax in the future, as well as ensure that the assets pass down through the generations. This type of bigger-picture planning requires the expertise of all three professions, so it is much better that they formulate a plan for the client together.

Instead of the client getting three sets of individual advice, the client gets better advice and also an easier life if these professionals are talking to each other first, and then putting together a cohesive strategy that benefits the client the most. As a result, where possible we always try to work closely with clients of other trusted advisers, so that we formulate a plan that achieves all their objectives in the best possible way. We call working together in this way 'the trusted team approach' and, as a result, we work with a number of firms of accountants, solicitors and specialist advisers to deliver a more comprehensive advice process for our clients. We are not looking to move them away from their existing advisers, but simply to work more closely with them to ensure the client gets the maximum value for their fees.

You may be wondering how this relates to your team of marketers working around the clock to find you clients. One of the benefits to this approach is that you end up working with other firms that also look after your ideal clients, but that aren't competing with you. For us, that is typically accountants, solicitors, estate agents and other professional advisers, but that may not be the case for your business. So, the first step is to identify other businesses that share your best-fit clients, but that are not competing with you in business.

The key to making this work is in the next steps. It is relatively easy to find other firms that will agree to do this in concept, but much more difficult to then actually make it work. You need to be clear what is in it for them. Is it adding value to their existing client service, a share of your fee or are they expecting referrals back? Make sure this is clear, and you can deliver, as sometimes it isn't easy to refer in the opposite direction.

For example, the architect can refer work to a builder, but rarely the other way around, as that work has normally been done before the builder enters the conversation. If the architect expects the referrals back and doesn't get them, eventually they will stop referring clients to you, so you need to address this at the outset. Perhaps they don't want a fee share, and you cannot refer back, so find something else. Is it a day out or offering your service for free? There is always something you can do, obviously taking care to avoid issues with the Bribery Act. If it is an activity or an experience, try and find something that allows you to build that relationship even stronger. A meal out, a day at a sports game or maybe a game of golf all works well here but find something that works for you. The important thing is to establish what motivates your introducers to refer clients to you and to make sure you deliver on that.

The next step to making sure the trusted team approach works for you is to demonstrate exactly what you do. In the first instance, this should be a presentation, already prepared, so that anytime you meet a potential trusted team partner, you can clearly present them with exactly what you do. It never ceases to amaze me the number of business owners and professionals that I meet where very few have a professional presentation that they can clearly show me.

You don't need to go through slide by slide, but having had a chat with them, you can use this as your visual material or as a memory aid. This presentation should be 90% visuals, with only a few slides that have words on them. They don't want to sit and read in front of you and, if they are, they aren't listening to you talk. Work on the basis that nothing smaller than a font size of 40, which will ensure you keep words to a minimum and pictures, graphics and charts make up the lion's share of your work. After all, a picture tells a thousand words.

When you meet with a potential trusted team partner, there is also a clear structure that works well in the meeting. I call this the trusted team meeting. Don't charge in guns blazing, desperate to get your presentation done and your polished pitch out there. First, they may be thinking the same, which means they aren't listening, and second, until you know more about them, how can you appeal to their greatest needs? Think back to Sir Alex Ferguson and Gazza, and the R-Factor Question from the Strategic Coach Program – "If we were sat here one year from now, what must have happened for you to be happy with the progress you have made?"

If, for example, you know they really want to grow their practice income, then guess what, you offering an introducer fee for referrals may well be their ticket to get there. We have also found it very helpful to have a brochure they can take away specifically aimed at the trusted team. They'll probably chuck it without reading it, but the quality of this brochure will give them a feel for the quality of the work you will be giving to their clients, so don't scrimp on it. Make it look professional. If you have written a book, make sure you give them a signed copy of that, too.

The trusted team meeting is a powerful start and, if you stop there, you may leave the meeting thinking you have cracked the nut, with the promise of a consistent flow of referrals. In my experience though, it rarely is enough. If you want to really make this a roaring success, there are a few more things you need to do.

The first is you need to make this a more compelling offer for their clients. The first meeting with a financial planner at Efficient Portfolio, what we call the Exploration Meeting, normally costs the client £197 if they come to us cold. However, if they come to us as an introduction from one of our trusted team partners, then we know they are more likely to be a better fit for our business. As a result, we waive the cost of this meeting. That means the trusted team partner can genuinely say to their clients that, as a result of them referring the client to us, the client will save £197. That makes the trusted team partner look great in the client's eyes, and also makes it more compelling for the client to follow their suggestion of meeting us. Win, win!

Second, when you meet the trusted team partner, just being told about what you can do for their clients is not enough. It is much more powerful if they see it first-hand. I'll come back to the 'unique business process' later in this book, so I won't go into detail here but, if it's appropriate, you need to get them to go through part or all the way through your unique business process if at all possible. The second stage of our unique business process is the 'efficient financial plan': a bespoke plan that allows clients to understand more about their current finances, see what their financial future looks like, and clearly understand what actions they can take today to turn that financial future into the one they want. We charge between £500 and £3,000 for the efficient financial plan, so it is a valuable document.

The best way for us to show a potential future trusted team partner how we can help their clients is to show them how we can help them. So, in addition to offering the partner a free Exploration Meeting worth £197, we will offer them, and their other business partners, a free efficient financial plan too, worth up to £3,000. That way they get to witness first-hand how we can improve what they are currently doing, how much clarity a lifetime cash-flow forecast can give them about their own financial future, and why we are different to any firm they have dealt with in the past.

This approach has two advantages. First, if your introducers understand how your unique business process helped them, they can better explain it to their clients, and can honestly say that they have been through it themselves. Second, if the introducers like what you do and your advice is relevant to them, there is a fair chance that they will go onto become a client of yours, too. You can still charge them for this, as this is generally where you start incurring the bigger costs and taking on much greater liability, so you don't necessarily want to be doing that without charging, but it will, of course, depend on your business. Maybe you can charge them favourable rates, but if they end up becoming a client or customer of yours as a result of liking what you do, that makes them even more likely to refer their clients to you. Not just because they understand it and see the benefit of what you do, but because they are probably now seeing you on a regular basis.

The next step to make this new trusted team relationship work is to follow on from that last point. Arrange regular times to meet to discuss hot topics in your business, any mutual clients that you have referred and, also importantly, case studies. If you bring a case study of a client you have helped, and they do the same, it gives you a great understanding of the ways that you both can help other clients. These regular meetings are then the springboard onto finding some new referrals for each other. We all know that normally following a meeting, we will all have an inbox full of emails, and a pile of work on our desks, so having to think up clients to refer would ordinarily take pride of place in the back seat, soon to be forgotten. Identifying specific actions and specific people in the meeting will mean that we can all focus our attention on the most important actions, which will lead to much greater success. So, schedule these regular meetings; at Efficient Portfolio, we aim to do them quarterly with our trusted team partners, to ensure the trusted team relationship blossoms; otherwise, it will wilt and die.

Another way to really get this working well for you is to identify how you can give value back to your trusted team partners. One way I have done this is by creating the 'Breakthrough Business Breakfast.' This is a free monthly breakfast meeting where I teach other business professionals, particularly accountants and solicitors, how they can find more clients, have a better work-life balance and enjoy their careers more.

At the Breakthrough Business Breakfast events, I get to share with my trusted team partners the sort of ideas that I am sharing with you in this book, but I can also do more. It is one thing reading a book but working with the author in a workshop format takes it to a whole new level. The learning and ideas that spring from the event can be far greater than you get when you read a book. In addition to thinking about how you can improve your own business, you can hear some of the ideas of like-minded professionals, and that can inspire you into new ideas too. It is also an opportunity to network with like-minded professionals, and to extend your own trusted team network. You are welcome to come and join us, if you would like. You can register for the next event at www.efficientportfolio.co.uk/events.

The final step to really make this relationship flourish is to plan some joint events and initiatives together. This could be a golf day, a seminar or a marketing exercise. If you have written your book, why not offer to give the trusted team free copies that they can send to their clients as a gift? It makes them look good and, simultaneously, they are sending around your 'big business card.' Another win-win situation.

The key to a strong trusted team relationship is finding those mutually beneficial situations. If in business you can find these moments, everyone walks away happy and motivated. If you drive too hard a deal, or like the builder and the architect expect it all one way, the relationship will soon fizzle out. Find the win-wins, and you will make a huge success. In my Better Future coaching, I get people to do an exercise to help them identify the members and the approach to use for their very own trusted team. You can find out more about this at www.charliereading.com/BF.

When you have other business owners and professionals on the lookout for your next clients, it really does oil the cogs of your business beautifully.

CHAPTER SUMMARY

- Identify other businesses that have the same clients as you, but that aren't in competition with you.

- Work out what it is they are most looking for.

- Build a trusted team of other business professionals so that you can create a far better solution for your clients, as well as refer clients to each other.

- Find ways to add as much value as possible to your trusted team to make the referrals flow.

CHAPTER 6

BUSINESS BY 'NUMBERS'

A few summers ago, a friend of mine, Dave, was over from the US. As an avid baseball and basketball fan, he asked if I would take him to a British sporting event. As it was during the summer, my options were limited, but I could get tickets to see England play in a one-day international at cricket. What better demonstration of a truly British sporting occasion?

It was shortly after the first over that he spotted the scoreboard. In a way that only an American could, he blasted, "What the hell is that thing when it's at home? Is that telling me the stats for the whole damn season?"

Have you ever seen a professional cricket scoreboard? If you follow cricket, the scoreboard makes complete sense. You know how many overs have been bowled and how many are left in the innings; you know which batsmen are in, how many runs they've scored, who's facing the next ball and how many more they need to win; you know the bowler's name, the number of balls left in the over, the runs scored and the wickets lost. All crucial information about the match that tells you who's winning, but to Dave, it was like looking at a Japanese textbook on brain surgery. He couldn't read the scoreboard, so he couldn't understand what was happening in the game.

Business is the same as sport, and particularly cricket. If you can't read the scoreboard, you don't know the score, and if you don't know the score, how can you tell who are the winners from the losers?

Many business owners I meet cannot read and understand their accounts. If they cannot read and understand their accounts, then they don't know what is going on. They don't know the score, and they don't know whether they are winning or losing. As a result, if you run your own business it is essential that you at least have a grasp of your balance sheet and your profit and loss. Even better, though, is to track your income versus your expenditures.

However, this chapter, and section of The Better Future Framework, isn't about knowing how to read your balance sheet and profit and loss (P&L), as important as that is. It is about knowing your most important numbers to your specific business, and not three months or even 12 months after the event but knowing them now.

Looking at your accounts three or even six months after the year has finished is a bit like trying to make a substitution half an hour after the game of cricket has ended. You could well have already lost the game by that stage. Even reviewing your accounts every three months with your accountant just isn't enough. That's like only assessing the game at half time and full time. You need to have your finger on the pulse of the game, and to do that you need weekly reporting of all your key results.

Whether you run your own company or are a partner or consultant in a bigger company, you need to know what your most important numbers are, and you need to keep track of them on a weekly basis. Let me explain what I mean.

At Efficient Portfolio, we build clients an efficient financial plan – their own bespoke document that contains analysis of their investment finances to see what's good and what's not, a lifetime cash-flow forecast that allows them to see what their financial future currently looks like, and then recommendations of what they need to do to achieve their goals. After our first meeting with the client, we build this plan for them, and it usually takes us around three months to complete. Once the client has read it, we meet them again and make sure they understand everything. Sometimes this takes an additional meeting or two to get everything finalized. It then may take us up to three more months to implement their wishes. That means that it can be up to nine months before we get to the end of that client journey, and also nine months before we get the lion's share of our fees.

As a result of this time frame, it is very easy to get caught up in what client work is happening at that time. For instance, one of the advisers may see a lot of new clients in January; in March they are busy reviewing the clients' finances; in April they are busy helping the paraplanner finish all the efficient financial plans; in May they are busy conducting the Planning Meetings; in July they are busy implementing the clients' desired outcomes; and then in September, they have nothing to do. That is, unless they know their numbers. If they know how many Exploration Meetings they need to do every week and every month, they know how to keep their client pipeline full. If they know what the average client brings in fees in their first year, they know how many Planning Meetings they need to have booked each month to hit their target.

But it doesn't stop there. Once the planning is agreed with the client, we send a suitability letter to confirm exactly which parts of the planning the client wanted to implement. If these start to build up because the team is busy, this can be a compliance problem for the business, so as the business owner, I need to know what that number is. Is it rising or falling? Is the weekly income more than the weekly expenditure this year, and how has that trend changed over the last quarter or year? After all, 'turnover is vanity, profit is for sanity, and cash-flow is reality.' What are the best months, on average, and what are the worst? Are complaints and quibbles becoming more of a problem? Is your customer satisfaction score rising or falling?

If you don't know the score, you don't know whether you are winning or losing. If you don't even have a scoreboard, what hope have you of knowing the score? As a result, you need to track your key business figures. Not on an annual basis through your accountant, because by the time you see that, it is too late. Even on a quarterly basis you are behind the times. You need to track these numbers on a weekly basis, so you can rectify problems immediately and maximize opportunities before they are lost.

One of my first jobs every Monday morning is to review our successful business scoreboard. It tells me nearly everything I need to know about the business in one line of data. It allows me to see whether the business is on track to hit its targets and if not, why. It allows me to see the length of the 'sausage machine,' it gives me the ability to predict cash flow and business in the months ahead, and it enables me to spot problems that may be building in the background. If you want to win at business, you need to know your numbers. You need to know, track and review your numbers every week, as this will put you in the driving seat of your business.

Your numbers may well be different to mine. You probably have a completely different business model to me, but you will have key stages in your client journey that you can track, ways you can track whether you are getting better or worse, and ways that you can see whether you are making more or less money than before. I have put a lot of time into refining mine, and it has evolved into a key part of our business. Later in this chapter, I'll show you how to create your very own successful business scorecard, using mine as a template. However, before we get to that stage, we need to know what your numbers are, so it's worth grabbing a pen and paper and starting to think about these now. This isn't about creating a huge and burdensome admin exercise for you, so please don't worry.

I'd like you to identify your key numbers. What do you need to keep track of to ensure you know how your business is running? Not only do you need to identify what numbers you need to know, you need to identify who on your team can track and complete these figures for you on a weekly basis.

Finally, you also need to identify a target for each number. Ideally, this should be a calculated figure; however, you may not be able to do this at this stage.

Here is an example. We need to keep track of how many referrals we get, how many first meetings we generate from these leads and how many of them become clients. Moreover, we also need to know how many new client meetings and referrals we need to hit our target. If our year's target is £1m of client fee income, and the average new client generates us £10,000 in fees in their first year, I know that to hit our target we need to be writing £19,230 worth of business each week. That means we need to take on roughly two new clients a week. But not everyone we meet becomes a client. I know that around 73% of Exploration Meetings yield new clients, as I have been tracking this for some time, so I now know that I actually need 2.7 Exploration Meetings per week to hit that. Of the referrals we get from different sources, I know that we convert 55% of them into Exploration Meetings. As a result, I know that if I want to write £1m of new business, I don't need 2.7 referrals per week, I actually need five. The great thing about this is that next year, if my target is £2m, unless I can generate more income per client or improve those percentages, I know I now need to be generating ten new referrals per week. Of course, you need to do both, and we'll come to that in due course, but at this stage, it is about knowing the score.

When you come to set your targets, you can either decide on how you can calculate a more specific target that will deliver the results you want, or initially this can be a gut feeling for what you think you need to achieve in that area to hit your annual targets. In time, as you track the numbers more closely, you will be able to set more accurate targets that will deliver the results you desire.

But Rome wasn't built in a day. I am on about our fifth version of our successful business scorecard. It is ever-evolving.

Not only that, but just by writing this section of the book, I have just identified another way we can make it even better. The clarity you will get on your business by looking at these figures each week is quite amazing. In less than five minutes, you can see every important aspect of your business and identify what needs to happen to hit your annual targets and get back on track if you are off. It will allow you to identify problems building in the business far earlier than before, and make sure you always have your finger on the pulse. In time, it will also allow you to work fewer hours and in a more flexible way, so you could also create a win-win situation.

In addition to knowing your numbers, you need to know where your referrals and clients and customers are coming from. We have a document that we call the referral register. Were they referrals from clients, introducers, seminars, your website? By knowing where your new clients are coming from, you can track which of your strategies is proving successful. There is no point in ploughing good money after bad or spending time with people who are not generating you the clients you thought they would.

Keeping track of where your referrals come from is really important but, to be really successful, we need to take it a step further. We need to look at where our best five clients each year came from. Take a look at the total earnings from your clients over the last 12 months and identify where each of them came from. This is important for a couple of reasons.

First, if you are getting your very best clients from one or two sources, you perhaps need to spend even more time nurturing those sources. If it is a particular introducer, could you spend more time with them to get even more of those best-fit clients? Could you take them out to dinner to thank them? If it is your website that is converting well, how could you get that in front of more people's eyes?

The second reason is it is important to know what the average earnings from your five best clients were. It is sensible to track this every year, so go back and look at how this changed in recent years. I hope you find it is getting higher each year. If it isn't, then perhaps you need to look into how you could make that figure higher next year.

Now that you know the average fee earned from your top clients over the last year, the final piece of the puzzle is to set your minimum client fee. It is often difficult when you meet someone who isn't your best-fit client to say no. A recent example in our business was when Henry, one of our financial planners at Efficient Portfolio, saw a client who couldn't afford to pay us for the advice he needed. Henry decided to waive the cost of our Efficient Financial Plan, in the hope that he would still get a £1,500 fee if the client wanted us to help him reorganize his pensions. As he said to me afterward, having invested the time in doing the Exploration Meeting and paid the cost of the marketing to attract him, it made sense to try and cover our costs by trying to generate £1,500 out of this client.

The problem is that this client will cost us a lot more than £1,500. The marketing cost and adviser time has already been lost. If Henry does the plan for free, and even if he does generate £1,500 in fee income, it will have cost us money. For the work that is needed to build the plan, to implement the ideas, to pay the professional indemnity insurance and regulatory fees associated with the advice, and the other costs associated with this work will easily amount to £1,500; however, that isn't the biggest problem. For every bit of time Henry spends looking after this client, that is time taken away from him when he could have been finding a best-fit client. While the £1,500 may mean we break even, it will more likely cost us around £10,000 in fees as he will not have found someone that is a best-fit client in that time.

You may be thinking at this stage what a cruel and heartless person Charlie is. This client needs their help, but cannot afford it and, therefore, they are going to shun him. Let's be honest, we are in business to make money. If we don't make money, we won't be here to help anyone. That said, that doesn't mean you shouldn't do some pro bono work as a way of giving back. We do this as part of our business; however, it is important we do it on a pre-determined number of occasions, otherwise you run the risk of running your business dry and not making any profit.

In my Better Future coaching, I get people to do an exercise to help them work on what that should look like. You can find out more about this at www.charliereading.com/BF.

You can download a copy of the successful business scorecard, which includes my referral register, from www.charliereading.com/SBS.

CHAPTER SUMMARY

- It is vital that you have your finger on the pulse of your business. If you don't know the score, you don't know if you are winning or losing.

- Create a successful business scorecard so that you know exactly what is happening in your business.

- You need to know what minimum fee income you will work for, plus also what fees your best clients are generating for you, so you can move the business forwards in the way you want.

CHAPTER 7

AMASS YOUR WEALTH

The final step to The Profitable Business P.L.A.N. is to 'Amass' as much of the money that you make as possible. It is all very well finding ways to make lots more money, but only if you then use it wisely will it allow you to create the future you want, both for you and your business. If you end up handing over huge chunks to the tax man, to below average financial products and to poor financial advisers, your efforts will be wasted.

Making the most of your money is, of course, my bread and butter. While I love helping people like you improve your business, my greatest expertise lies in helping you create a better financial future for you and your loved ones. I realize as a business owner that you are often so focused on making money within your business that you give the money you make, and particularly the money you have withdrawn from the business, even less attention. We need to change that now.

You know your business, but do you understand how to make the most of your money? You may have a pension, and maybe even a financial adviser, but do you know whether you are on track to have enough money for the future you want? Will you be able to afford to retire when and how you want to? Will you be able to afford to fulfil the bucket-list goals that you have been promising yourself? Will you be able to afford to live where you want to in retirement? Will you be able to afford to pass your business down to the next generation if they want to be involved? Will you be able to create a legacy, rather than just leaving a few items in a will?

This chapter isn't a comprehensive account of what you can do with your money; it is designed to be more about the concepts around what you need to do to become financially free in the future. There are some amazing opportunities that only a business owner has, so I'll highlight these along the way. Finally, I don't want you to think that implementing all this stuff needs to take up a lot of your time. In fact, later in this chapter I'll show you how you can take a huge stride to improving your financial future in just four minutes.

Having worked in the financial services industry since 1999, I have discovered that there are six key steps to creating and maintaining a truly happy financial future. They are as follows:

1. PREPARE

Prepare, not repair!

Would you agree that the current £168 a week (correct as of 2019) that the government provides you with in retirement is not going to be enough to live on? In fact, imagine trying to live your current lifestyle on that amount of money. If you do not save enough for your retirement, that is what is going to end up happening to you. And here's the thing my industry really isn't very good at teaching people, and that's the psychology or mechanism around saving, which is probably one of the keys to your success. Financial advisers will tell you that you need to save and to set up a pension, but they often don't tell you the secrets to amazing financial success, which is all about the systems and psychology you use, not the products. Good financial planning is also about mitigating the risks of unexpected events that can derail your plan in the future.

At Efficient Portfolio, I created **The S.M.A.R.T. Saving Solution** to ensure our clients can prepare properly for their retirement. This is how we have helped our clients build their very own **S.I.M.P.L.E. Money Management Method** – a system that allows them to ensure that they are saving the right amounts for different areas of their life in a nearly effortless way that makes the maximum impact on their lifestyle and future.

In order to get to financial freedom as quickly as possible, you need to understand a number of key financial principles; an example of this is compound growth. Let me explain with a story. My friend Chris lives in Singapore. When he was visiting me a few years ago, we decided to play some golf. Chris is an investment banker so, as the reputation goes, is a little reckless with money. On the other hand, I need to be cautious with money. Walking up the first tee, Chris said we ought to be playing this golf match for money. "Chris," I said, "I do not need any extra reason to play bad golf, so please, let's not."

"Charlie," he said, "you are a successful businessman, and I am sure you can cope with playing golf for a little money."

"If we must, but let's just play for 10p per hole."

"10p per hole sounds a little pathetic," he said. "Let's do that but double it each hole."

"OK," I reluctantly agreed.

On the first hole, which I think I lost, we were playing for 10p, but hey, as he says, I'm a successful businessman, and I'm sure I can cope with that. On the second hole we were playing for 20p, not too much stress there either, and 40p on the third and 80p on the fourth are also fine with me. By the seventh, though, we are playing for £6.40 a hole, and it quickly started getting out of hand from there on in.

By the tenth hole we were playing for £51 per hole, and that was too much for me, so I called the betting a day. But it certainly made me think about what was going to happen if we continued. By the 16th, we would have been playing for £3,276, and on the 18th we would have been playing for £13,104. Despite the earlier machismo, this was way too big for either of us to be entertaining.

The increasing amounts I've just told you about are what is known as compound growth. It is the effect of the growth on the growth on the growth. To look at it another way, if you took a standard piece of paper (0.05mm thick) and folded it in half 50 times, do you know how high it would reach? The answer is about 100 million kilometres, which is about two thirds of the distance between the Sun and the Earth. Amazing, isn't it! That is compound growth at work.

If you can get your money benefiting from compound growth, you will reach financial freedom more quickly, and stay there for longer, so you need to find ways to get a bit more growth out of your money at every opportunity.

As a business owner, you have some unique opportunities and also some unique risks. For example, you can extract money directly from your company into your pension, and save paying income tax, corporation tax and National Insurance tax on this money. You can use the money in your pension to purchase a commercial property that you can rent back to your business, which means that your company is then paying rent to your pension. That pension is also secure in the situation where your business runs into financial difficulty. Your pension can loan money back to your company, and it can also borrow.

As a business owner, you can control the amount of tax you pay through the amount and structure of your drawings, and you can use investment tax wrappers to shelter larger drawings from the tax man. You can leave money in the business and benefit from entrepreneur's relief or reduce your tax by drawing the money out at a lower rate once you have retired. You have flexibility to create an amazing financial strategy to get you to financial freedom as quickly as possible and give you the opportunity to stop working, if you wish.

However, as a business owner, you have more risks than an employee. For example, if you are sick, have an accident or even worse, die, you need to ensure that you and your loved ones have enough money for their future. That needs to be income to pay the bills, whatever they are, and capital to pay for upfront costs. One of the most valuable things I do as a financial planner is to help our clients see the financial shortfalls they have and fill those gaps with the necessary protection.

In addition to these, though, the business owner has other considerations to think about. What happens if a key member of the staff suffers the same fate? Could your opportunity to hit your targets be lost? Could key relationships be lost if that were to happen, with clients or even your bank? Key person protection ensures you have the means to deal with these scenarios, if they occur.

Also, do you own the business with someone else? If they die and leave their shares to their partner, children or parents, how will that affect your business? Do you want to run the business with their beneficiary, and do they even want to be in that situation? Ideally you want to buy them out but will you have the funds? If the boot was on the other foot, wouldn't your beneficiary want the money rather than the shares? Shareholder protection or partnership protection makes sure who needs the shares gets them, and who needs the money gets that.

2. PLAN
If you are failing to plan, you are planning to fail.

Probably the biggest concern people have in the lead-up to retirement is the uncertainty over whether they will run out of money later on in life. Another key concern is not knowing if they will be able to do the things they want to. On the flip side of that is feeling too worried to spend, thus ending up becoming the richest person in the graveyard.

The key to a successful retirement is being able to look into the future, see what you need, and then plan how you can get there, including what you can afford today. 'A goal is just a dream with a deadline' and that could not be more poignant than when it comes to retirement.

You'd think this would be covered by most financial advisers, but it generally isn't. Financial advisers tend to focus on the products and the advice around them. A small minority of our industry, at the point of writing, has taken this a huge step further and embraced financial planning.

The approach most people take to their finances is to only look at the next road sign, not the bigger picture.

This sounds obvious, doesn't it, but in actual fact most people go through their lives not really knowing what their financial futures look like. They can see what they have now, and how their decisions have affected their money in the past by looking in the rear-view mirror, but they do not look further ahead. In order to get to your destination, you need to plan the journey at the start, so you have an idea of how you are going to get there.

As a result, when it comes to their finances, people get lost, and most don't get to where they wanted to go. Where they do end up isn't where they wanted to be at all, because of the odd wrong turn along the way, and while they are not a million miles away from where they wanted to be, to undo those wrong turns isn't quick and easy.

When it comes to your finances, what is your map? It is known as a lifetime cash-flow forecast. A lifetime cash-flow forecast gives you the clarity of what your financial future will look like. It projects your life forwards, allowing you to build in the aspects that are important to you, so that you can see how they will impact your financial future. It allows you to make more informed decisions because you can see the impact they will have on your future.

To allow you to see where you are going with your money, it isn't just a case of removing the blindfold or looking forwards out of the window screen. You need to imagine that your life, from here to the end, is a timeline. Lifetime cash-flow forecasting enables you to visualize your future wealth and see how the decisions you make today will affect your wealth over time. It is vital in financial planning, as it helps you gain greater clarity around your financial future.

The lifetime cash-flow forecast gives you clarity on your financial future, but that is just one piece of the jigsaw.

In order to help our clients see their financial future more clearly, we created **The S.A.F.E. Retirement Roadmap** so that we could help them clarify what their financial future looks like and be able to forecast different scenarios, because this gives them the confidence to make the right financial decisions for their desired future.

Do you think you would benefit from knowing more clearly about your financial future? If you do, we have also built a very basic version of the lifetime cash-flow forecast that you can play around with for free at www.efficientportfolio. co.uk/tools/life-time-cash-flow-forecast/.

The S.A.F.E. Retirement Roadmap is, however, about much more than just the lifetime cash-flow forecast. That is the cornerstone of it, but it is also about better understanding your current finances, i.e. what bits are good and what bits aren't and, therefore, need improving. It is also looking into the future, because only once you have a clear idea of what you want in the future can a financial planner really help. So, let's take a look at what is important to you in the future.

In order that you can create a better financial future, I have put together an exercise for you to work through. This can be found in *The Entrepreneurial Happiness Workbook*, which you can download for free from www.charliereading.com/EH.

3. PROFIT

This is growth over and above inflation.

Saving money is important but, if you do not get that money working harder for you, then you will have to save twice as much, for twice as long and it will run out twice as quickly, so you need to allow your savings to generate a profit. What do I mean by profit? No, not the same as profit for your business, but similar. There is a saying that goes, "Turnover is vanity, but profit is sanity." The same applies to your personal money.

Surprisingly, the amount of interest or growth you are getting is not the important figure. The essential figure is how much more growth/interest are you getting above inflation. If you are getting 8% growth that may sound brilliant, but if inflation is 10%, you just lost 2% of your money. If you get 3% growth on your money that may sound rubbish, but if inflation was negative at 2% deflation, you just got 5% growth, which may well be good for you. What I therefore mean by profit, in this instance, is getting your money to grow faster than inflation.

That means that the buying power is going down every year. As a result, you need to get that money working hard for you, rather than you working harder for it. You need to be benefiting from as much growth as possible to get the process of compound growth really working for you, as I pointed out earlier in this chapter.

At Efficient Portfolio, I created **The R.A.D.I.C.A.L. Investment Approach** – a seven-step process that helps our clients feel more confident that they are getting the best returns possible, for a level of risk that they are comfortable with. Ensuring their money is growing over and above inflation, but without gradually getting riskier and riskier as happens naturally in a portfolio, is a critical.

As a business owner, this doesn't just apply to the money you have extracted from your business into your pension or your own savings and investments. Most successful businesses retain a level of capital in the company they never really intend to use, just in case they need it in the future. This money usually sits in a bank account doing nothing apart from being eroded by inflation over time. While it is important to seek advice for your specific situation, there is usually no reason not to invest some of this money to ensure that it is at least keeping pace with inflation, if not growing above it.

4. PENSION

You need to create a dynamic income that matches your lifestyle.

As and when you get to retirement, you need to turn the capital you have saved into an income. You could, of course, hand all those savings over to one company in exchange for a low but guaranteed level of income for the rest of your life. However, the flat rates on these products are calculated on the assumption that you are as likely to climb Mount Kilimanjaro at 95 as you are at 65, and we all know that isn't the case. The restrictions on these products can mean that if you don't live long into retirement, your family cannot benefit from what is left over.

Since George Osbourne introduced the Pension Freedom legislation, there is more flexibility than ever before but with flexibility comes complexity. The decisions you make with your savings, investments and particularly your pension when you reach retirement make a massive difference to your life thereafter, so it is vital you make the right decisions to maximize your money and your life.

Having worked hard to save this money, making the right decisions at this stage will impact how you live the rest of your life, so it is vital you get it right. In order to address this, we created **The D.R.E.A.M. Income Strategy** to ensure that you maximize your hard-earned savings and turn them into a flexible dynamic income that can deliver what you want, when you want.

As an example, a few years ago a new client came to me when he was being forced to retire earlier than expected. He was 63, and it was too late in life to be going out and looking for another job doing what he did; plus, he hadn't planned to retire until he reached a specific financial milestone, and he needed another two years to get there. He was devastated, as he felt he had let his family down. He had promised his wife a new kitchen, regular trips abroad to see their children, and he felt he could no longer deliver on those promises.

Using the tools and systems in The D.R.E.A.M. Income Strategy we were able to show him how he could deliver on the retirement he had pledged. He could have everything he wanted and more, just by making the right decisions around his money.

Business owners often want to retire gradually, so building an income that can be phased as your income reduces is essential to avoid paying too much tax. The D.R.E.A.M. Income Strategy can ensure you get the biggest bang for your buck from those hard-earned savings.

5. PROGRESS
Evolving with you, rather than stagnating.

If you get prepared in the right way, create a clear plan for the future, get your money growing faster with less risk, and create the right income for when you stop working, that will be great. However, will it still be right by this time next year? Probably not. There will be changes in your situation, the economy, legislation, the markets and the options available, which mean that you need to make changes to ensure your financial planning evolves with you, rather than gradually stagnating, as all too often is the case.

And this is the area where my industry seriously falls down. Much of the financial services sector only wants to see you again if they think they can sell you something else. For those who do see you, generally they focus on the basic investment performance and nothing more. A proper review process needs to be so much more than that. It needs to look again into your financial future, new tax planning opportunities, how much you are spending/saving, as well as assessing the investments.

That's why, soon after I launched Efficient Portfolio in 2006, I developed **The Progressive Review Programme**. As a client, you want to have the peace of mind that your money is still working as hard for you as possible and is evolving and adapting to an ever-changing life.

This process is unique to us and is the reason why many clients leave their current financial adviser to join us. We deliver a review service like no other in ways that allow us to do so much more to ensure your financial planning actually does evolve with you, rather than gradually grinding to a halt.

As a business owner, there is even more legislation to think about, and of course you have your business environment and trading conditions to think about too. This creates problems and opportunities, and so it is essential that your financial planning evolves within this ever-changing landscape. The Progressive Review Programme is how we help our clients do this.

6. PERSONAL
It's about more than just the money.

I've been talking about money for a little while now, but I am sure you would agree that there is more to a happy financial future than just money.

Historically, people considered power and money to be the keys to success, but what good does power and money do if you don't have wellbeing? If you don't have your health, and people around you whom you love, then can you really be described as successful? When it comes to your financial future, the same applies. It is all very well focusing on the money side of retirement, but you also need to consider what to do with your time and how you maintain and even improve your wellbeing.

That is why we created **The Fulfilled Life Formula**. This is how we help our clients do much more than just create a safe financial future. It is how we create a legacy, rather than just leaving material possessions in a will. As an example, when you own your own business, you can usually leave that business to your children free of inheritance tax. Sounds good, doesn't it? But let's think about what that means. First, if something happens to you and your spouse during your children's younger years, they will inherit a lot of money the day they turn 18. Now that may lead to an amazing freshers' week, but probably not a good life thereafter. Whether they just waste it, lose it through marrying the son- or daughter-in-law from hell, or worse, let it ruin their life, that probably isn't what you want. Also, once the business is sold, whether that be by your spouse or children, that money will now be liable to 40% inheritance tax when it passes down through the generation.

By using a trust framework, you can ringfence that money to protect against these risks and allow your future generations to thrive. The Fulfilled Life Formula is how we do that for our clients.

We call these six steps to creating a better financial future **The Efficient Money Method**.

HOW CAN WE HELP?

There is obviously a lot to cover here, and I wanted to give you the basic stepping stones to creating a better financial future, but this isn't the book to go into more detail. If, however, you would like to learn more about how we help business owners, we regularly host a webinar called 'The Entrepreneurs Guide to Financial Planning,' which you can register for at www.efficientportfolio.co.uk/events. It may be that a webinar is not your thing, so if you'd rather come and meet us in person at one of our events, visit www.efficientportfolio.co.uk/Events to register.

Finally, in 2018 we developed **'The 2 Minute Retirement Plan'** – a mini financial plan that takes just two minutes to complete. This is completely free of charge and gives you an indication of what your future could look like. Take a huge step towards creating a better financial future for yourself by visiting www.efficientportfolio.co.uk/2MRP.

Remember, if you are failing to plan, you are planning to fail.

CHAPTER SUMMARY

- You need to ensure you get your business profits working as hard as possible and allowing you to become financially free outside your company. You can do this by following six key steps, which we call **The Efficient Money Method**.

- **PREPARE**: Understand the psychology and systems that allow you to get to financial freedom as quickly as possible. Prepare, not repair.

- **PLAN**: Have a clear vision of what your financial future looks like and understand the impact that the decisions you make today will have on your future. If you're failing to plan, you're planning to fail.

- **PROFIT**: Get your money growing over and above inflation, working harder for you so you don't have to work for it. Get the best returns possible for a level of risk you are comfortable with.

- **PENSION**: Once you reach financial freedom, you need to make the right decisions in order to create a dynamic income that will deliver the life you desire.

- **PROGRESS**: Things change over time, and your finances are no different. You need to ensure that your financial planning evolves with you, rather than stagnating over time.

- **PERSONAL**: Life is about more than just the money. If you get it right, you can create an amazing lifestyle for you and the people you love. Create a legacy, not just a will.

SECTION 2

THE
FREE LIFE
BUSINESS
M.O.D.E.L.

THE FIVE-STEP GUIDE TO MAKING MORE TIME IN YOUR BUSINESS LIFE.

M   Magnify

O   Operations

D   Delegate

E   Energy

L   Life

CHAPTER 8

MAGNIFY YOUR MOVES

"If everything's under control, you're not going fast enough."
– Mario Andretti

If you want to create a better work-life balance, then you need to work out ways to magnify the work you do. If you can complete one piece of work but allow many people to benefit from it, two amazing things happen. First, you can make more money in less time. Second, and perhaps more importantly, you can help more people than you would have been able to previously, and potentially they can pay less for that help, too. Everyone is happy. The question is, how can you do this?

ONE TO MANY

Many businesses, like my own, involve spending a lot of time with clients on a one-to-one basis. The traditional model is to go out and try to meet lots of new clients, spend your time with those potential clients while you try to show them the value of your service, and then hope to continue to see them regularly in order to try to provide them with an ongoing service. All this involves a lot of time and, as I have already talked about earlier in this book, we only have so much time to work with. So how can you achieve more in less time?

One of the best ways is to identify how you can change your business from a one-to-one business to a one-to-many business. How can you pitch to many potential clients at once? How can you service many clients at the same time? Let me give you a few examples, initially of my business, but of some others too.

At Efficient Portfolio, we want to educate people about their money because by knowing and understanding more, they are more inclined to act to improve their financial future. As a result, one of our marketing approaches is The Wealth Workshop. By public speaking, I can build trust, educate and then essentially pitch our proposition to many people all at once. By taking the one-to-many approach, in one day I can generate enough new clients for several of our advisers, as well as giving a better financial education to those people who need it.

One of the biggest problems our industry has is the ongoing servicing of existing clients. Much of our industry still works on the basis that the adviser only wants to see you if they think they can sell you something new, not to service what you already have. Part of the reason for this is because otherwise, over time, they get bogged down with seeing existing clients, and they have no time to see new clients, which is where they make more of their money from.

As a result, you either get the advisers who don't want to provide ongoing service at all, so they can see plenty of new clients, or you get advisers who cap the number of clients that they look after and see no one new. Neither are ideal situations.

When I set up Efficient Portfolio, I was determined to provide a good ongoing service to our clients. Initially, having a good support team around me was enough, but after a while I realized there still needed to be more innovation. As a result, we introduced the client review workshop. We split the review into two elements: the client-specific content, like the changes happening in their life, and the aspects that applied to most clients, like investment performance, planning opportunities, legislation changes and some more interesting things like your 'bucket list.' All of the elements that applied to most people we now cover in the client review workshop, to a room full of clients. This gives us more time to cover generic issues in a cohesive fashion and ensure that the private meetings are far more focused and meaningful. I also spend far less time conducting reviews but achieve better results and client satisfaction.

By introducing the wealth workshop and the client review workshop, I have massively increased the number of people

I can help, thus making the business more profitable and my clients more confident, educated and, ultimately, feeling more secure about their futures. It may not always go perfectly, and in some cases it may not always be as good as seeing someone one-to-one, but the significant increase in what we can achieve motivates me to continue to innovate and make the process even better than one-to-one over time. That is certainly my experience.

Let's look at another person who has transformed their business by employing the one-to-many approach, to show that the method translates to other sectors.

James Dewane had been in the electrical industry for just over 25 years, having served his apprenticeship in a small family firm in Ireland. While he had a great career as an electrician, it was not without its ups and downs. In 2007 he had a thriving company, nine staff, three vans, a car and a shop front – only to find himself on the brink of personal bankruptcy because two developers he was working with went out of business, owing him a lot of money. Although he appeared to have a great turnover, the business was not profitable, so he could not recover from the failure. He had no choice but to start again.

He threw himself into learning how to market direct to the consumer by taking courses and reading books, and he managed to create a brand-new business within the domestic sector, but he was still exchanging time for money, and there was only so much time in the week. He decided to rethink his approach. He decided to help other electricians market their business, using all the tools he had learned. He put down his tools and started speaking at events where his audience was 'the competition.' He has used the one-to-many approach to create a far more profitable, less time-intensive business that ultimately means he reaches a much wider audience.

One of the most influential people who has helped and mentored me in the public speaking space is the legendary

Andy Harrington. I attended his Public Speakers University and went on to also do his Elite course, which, among other things, meant a week's training with Andy and a team of coaches in Dubai. If you ever want to get better at something, find the best coach you can, and then totally immerse yourself in their work. If you do that, you will make such huge strides forwards in short spaces of time, it will have a massive impact on your business and life.

So that is what I did: total immersion. If you want to improve your public speaking, I know of no one better to teach you than Andy Harrington. You can find out more at www.efficientportfolio.co.uk/AndyHarrington. It was thanks to Andy's help that I became an award-winning speaker.

UNIQUE BRANDED SOLUTION (UBS)

One of the things that Andy taught me was that to teach people from the stage, you need to create a system. It is no good trying to teach people the 101 things they need to know about your sector to be successful; you need to break it down into manageable chunks. If I ask you to remember those 101 things, you have no chance, but if I ask you to remember six systems, you have a much better chance. Within each of those systems, you can then remember the steps needed.

The Better Future Framework is an example of a Unique Branded Solution (UBS). So is The Efficient Money Method that I teach at The Wealth Workshop. By breaking it down into bite-sized chunks, it makes it easier for the audience to remember and understand, whether you are delivering it through video, the web or in person. It doesn't just benefit the receiver; it also benefits you in many ways too.

A well-thought-out UBS will force you to refine your thoughts and pick out the most important elements. It will ensure you package the most relevant pieces together.

It will mean that you have built your own unique intellectual product, something that no other business can offer, differentiating you from your competitors on a factor other than price. This last point is really important if what you do differently from your competitors comes down to price alone; there will always be someone who will do it cheaper, so the price will continue to fall.

Creating your own UBS gives you a unique product that no one else can compete with on a like-for-like basis. Not only that, but it is intellectual property like this that makes your business more valuable. Finally, when it comes to presenting the content, the system makes what you do a lot more memorable. As a result, you will be able to present without notes, one of the keys to becoming a successful speaker.

There are lots of aspects to creating your own UBS and, to do it justice, you'd be well advised to attend Andy's Public Speakers University; however, here is my quick-fire approach to creating a memorable UBS.

1. List all of the most important areas of what you do.
2. Ideally using a mind-mapping software (such as iMindMap), group them into areas. No fewer than three, no more than eight.
3. For each of these steps, identify the pain you are trying to remove for people, the area where you help them. For example, in regard to creating financial freedom, we help people prepare, plan, create profit, create a pension, progress and also help with the personal side of their finances too. You'll notice that all steps of my UBS begin with the letter 'P'; alliteration or acronyms are not essential, but they make your UBS punchier and more memorable.
4. Split each step into stages (i.e. their component parts) and name each of these areas. If you want to employ

the literary techniques I've mentioned, an online thesaurus is a great help. Alliteration and acronyms will make the stages of your UBS easier for you and your audience to remember and make them more phonetically pleasing.

5. Design a graphic that illustrates these areas. Here is The Efficient Money Method as an example.

THE EFFICIENT MONEY METHOD™

Source: Efficient Portfolio

STORIES

The economist **Josef Zweimüller** of the University of Zurich co-authored a study that found that early retirement, as much as we may crave it, seems to be bad for our health.

"[A]mong blue-collar workers, we see that workers who retire earlier have a higher mortality rate and these effects are pretty large."[2]

He drew this conclusion from assessing two very similar sets of blue-collar workers in Austria, where a change in the unemployment insurance system presented a unique opportunity for the study. This policy change allowed older workers in eligible regions to retire up to 3.5 years earlier than comparable workers in non-eligible regions. The programme generated substantial variation in the actual retirement age, which, arguably, was driven only by financial incentives and not driven by differences in individuals' health status. This let them examine the causal impact of early retirement on mortality.

The study showed that for every extra year of early retirement, workers lost about two months of life expectancy. This is not the first study to show a strong relationship between early retirement and earlier death, so we can draw the conclusion that we aren't actually very good at retirement. The old saying of 'working yourself into an early grave' should perhaps be revised.

I found this fascinating, as while we crave stopping work early, it is actually bad for us! I suppose, in retirement, every day is a Saturday, so there is no reason not to have that extra glass of wine, that pizza for tea, or have that lie in.

I use this story to introduce why I wrote *The Dream Retirement*. I used it in the book, and I have used it in radio interviews since. Every time I find an interesting story with an interesting angle or link to an aspect of what I do, I add it to my story database. That way, every time I talk or write about that subject, I can introduce it with a 'sticky story.' A sticky story literally 'sticks' with the audience and holds resonance with them.

Having a database of stories is a really powerful thing. When you get the opportunity to speak, explain a key concept, write a blog or record a video, you can make it more impactful with a sticky story.

The most important story of all is your own. The one that makes you the expert. When Andy Harrington talks about it, he refers to it as your 'expert positioning story.' If I am given the opportunity to talk to an unfamiliar audience, in most instances I need to explain who I am and why they should listen to me. If I don't, they will have a lot of unanswered questions, and they will also question why they should respect my opinion. You should, therefore, always be armed with a compelling expert positioning story, for whenever the need arises.

You might even have different variations of this story for different audiences. At the start of this book I told you a bit of my expert positioning story: the meeting with Uncle Bill, the Dickens Process at Unleash the Power Within and having my first book, *The Dream Retirement*, published. I could have provided a timeline of what I'd done throughout my career, but it would have been really dull. Making it into a story makes it much more interesting for the reader because it creates more emotion and, as a result, it makes it more memorable. It takes the reader or listener on a journey.

Stories are one of the oldest mediums in the world. Before we had YouTube, blogs or even books, we passed on our wisdom from one generation to another using stories. Sitting around the campfire, these stories were there to provide a learning lesson.

For your expert positioning story, you will need structure. You need to identify which of your key stories can be combined to make one longer and more impactful narrative. Work on it.

In my Better Future coaching, I get people to do an exercise to help them build their own expert story. You can find out more about this at www.charliereading.com/BF.

When you get the chance to tell your story, it is often an excellent business opportunity, so have it planned, practised and polished. Prior preparation prevents poor performance.

DO IT ONCE, USE IT MANY TIMES!

The reason for building a good directory of stories is so that you can reuse the same material time and time again. You can massively magnify your business success by using the 'do it once, use it many times' approach.

When Caryl and I first got together, I must have been a lot more romantic than I am now, because after just six weeks of dating, I whisked her away to Venice for her birthday. We had a wonderful few days walking the streets of the spectacular city, exploring things like the Ponte di Rialto, Basilica di San Marco and all the wonderful markets, shops, buildings and restaurants you can find by aimlessly wandering the labyrinth of side streets. Because of this trip, we said we would go back to Venice for our tenth anniversary. We tried to refamiliarize ourselves with the map to try and work out where we had been, to find the best restaurants online and tried to speak to friends who we knew had been there. As a result of all this research, we had a wonderful trip back to Venice.

My point here is that, had I written up just a little of our experiences the first time around, it would have been much easier to track down some of the things we wanted to revisit. In addition, over the years that passed since our first visit, we would have been able to help others visiting Venice to really enjoy their experience to the full.

Following on from our second visit, I knew at least two other couples who were going to be heading to Venice for a similar visit, and I knew they were going to ask us for recommendations. As a result, what I should have done the first time, but did do the second time, was write up a list of top tips for Venice. It didn't take long, and it ensures that if we go back again for our 20th wedding anniversary, we can remember what we did, where we stayed and where we ate from our previous visit. What has been done once will be used many times. The impact it then has is far greater for the same amount of effort.

There are lots of ways you can do this in your business. If you record a video, as well as using it as one video, can you break it down into chunks to make it into smaller videos too. You could transcribe that video into text and turn it into a blog article, something for your newsletter or for your website. You could extract the audio and turn it into a podcast. You could use the text from this video and add it to the text of other videos to make your next book, and you could then turn that into an audiobook or even an online course. One video will create masses of content if you choose to recycle it in different ways. You could even hire someone to follow you around, document what you talk about, and turn that into content. That's content without it costing you any time at all, which as we know, is our more valuable resource.

If you write a piece of text for a client, maybe in an email or in a report, that can become the basis of a blog article or newsletter. Or perhaps an advertorial in the local magazine? Every piece of content that gets produced by you and your business should have you thinking about how you can use it again and again.

Building a database of stories is the same thing. Speaking to many people rather than to one person is making you work one-to-many. Create web-based content that people can consume time and again, and you are at it again.

Look at the expertise you have and what you do on a day-to-day basis, and work out how you could do it once, to magnify the results you get from your efforts.

2. Source: https://freakonomics.com/2012/01/17/retirement-kills-a-new-marketplace-podcast/.

CHAPTER SUMMARY

- Help more people in less time by identifying ways that you can deliver what you do to many people at once, rather than just one-to-one. Whether that means through digital marketing or public speaking, leverage what you do with your time.

- Give people a clear message of what you do by creating a UBS, a system full of your intellectual property so that you can easily share it through a variety of different mediums.

- Get more traction with your message by identifying stories that help you more easily explain things in a more memorable way. As a business, use them time and again.

- Make an impact and build trust with your audience by building an Expert Positioning Story so that every time you need to explain where you have come from, and why your audience should trust you, you have a polished message that portrays what you need it to.

- Achieve more by building everything with a view to using it many times.

CHAPTER 9

OUTSTANDING OPERATIONS

I once read about a new managing director of a world-famous sweet factory. After years of success, the company's profits had been gradually slipping, and the new MD was brought in to reenergize the business. His first action was to look at the recipe involved in making the world-famous sweets, and he saw that there were 40 different ingredients. This seemed like a huge list of ingredients for such a tiny product, so he asked the confectioners to make a number of different versions of the sweet, and in each one to drop one ingredient.

After trying all the versions, the new MD identified the version that had no marked impact on the flavour and set about making the new recipe with the one less ingredient. The company immediately reduced its costs, increased its efficiencies and, after only a couple of months, the benefit to the company's bottom line was evident. The MD calls his confectioners in again and asks them to repeat the exercise. Again, the variation with one less ingredient but no noticeable impact to the flavour is selected, and the recipe readapted again. Sure enough, the benefits to the bottom line are seen just a few short months later. So, he repeats the exercise again, and again, until the recipe is just 30 ingredients and at its most profitable.

This seems like a powerful formula for success: give the customers the same experience while reducing costs each time, which should mean increasing your profits. However, a year on from the changes, the company started to see sales falling. The now-well-established and highly praised MD could not fathom why this was happening. At each stage there had been no marked change in the flavour, but people were now buying fewer of their sweets. Why would this be? The MD opened a pack of the original sweets, those that were produced before any changes were made and was blown away by its flavour. He then popped one of his new simplified sweets into his mouth and was amazed at the lack of flavour. How had this happened? There was no noticeable difference at each stage, but the compounded effect of these changes had made a huge impact.

And therein lies the problem. In business, we often come up with great ideas, but as that idea is handed from one employee to the next, the message gradually gets lost or forgotten. In business it is often easy to find great ideas that work, but over time we stop doing them. Usually not intentionally, but perhaps because of a staff change or perhaps because you get too busy. Over time, what was once a brilliant piece of work loses its sparkle. Just like the sweets, over the shorter timeframes there is no noticeable difference, but when compounded over a longer timeframe, the difference is huge.

According to Michael Gerber, a business owner needs an 'entrepreneur,' a 'manager' and a 'technician,' We all have elements of each in us, but we will always feel a strong bias to one of those areas. Identifying at an early stage what I was and what I wasn't – was a powerful learning point. Later, at Tony Robbins' Business Mastery program, he talked about it in similar terms but instead describing 'the technician' as 'the artist.'

CLONE YOURSELF

In the words of a solicitor I know, "To really allow the business to grow, you need to clone yourself." This is achieved by creating Outstanding Operations or processes, which deliver repeatable service from anyone in your business.

When I hired my first employee, my initial problem was to work out how I got across to her all the things that needed doing to build a client's plan following the initial meeting. I ended up creating a document called 'meeting follow up.' It certainly isn't rocket science, but that document has evolved over the years into something we still use with every new client.

I initially thought that the magic was in me creating my own processes, and people following them. How wrong I was. The magic is what happens after you delegate them. If you get it right, you'll end up delegating the role to someone who is better at that role. That was the key to the success of so many amazing entrepreneurs, including Steve Jobs, Henry Ford and Richard Branson.

In the words of Richard Branson, "People are a company's biggest asset, and in order for a business to survive and grow, a leader must learn to delegate duties effectively. I learned very early in my career that one of the smartest things a leader can do is hire people who excel in areas they are weaker in."

Over time, the people you delegate to will continue to improve how the process is completed. It's pivotal that you ask them to continually update the documented process, so that over the course of time, they turn your operations manual into Outstanding Operations.

This all sounds brilliant, but do you really need to bother with documenting it all? Isn't that just more work? It is more work, but it is some of the most valuable work that you will ever do. When someone is off sick, leaves the company or is promoted, it is this document that keeps the process happening. When we take on a new member of staff or move an employee to a new role, one of the first things we do is ask them to read the relevant section of this document. It ensures they can get up to speed in their role much more quickly and far more effectively.

Just because something has always been done in a particular way doesn't mean it should continue to be done that way. The process of delegating will allow you to find even more efficient ways to complete that role, because rather than just doing it as you have always done, it forces you to think about the best way to do that specific role.

Having the Outstanding Operations manual will ensure your business delivers more predictable results to your clients, and it will ensure that your business is more secure in the event of something unexpected happening to you or one of your team. In addition to this, it will make your business more valuable. The intellectual property (IP) that is contained within that document is what makes you unique. Someone buying that business can see how that can be continued after you have left, if it is clearly documented.

So, ensure you have clearly documented the Outstanding Operations manual for everything that happens in your business and make sure that the documented processes are revisited regularly so that they evolve with your business. When someone new joins your business, make sure they use that document as their guide and as the basis for their training and note taking, and ask them to add any missing areas as they go. That way, all the things they learn in their first few weeks that have been missed from the manual will be added for future joiners.

All this might sound like a lot of work, but it doesn't need to be. Here are some top tips on how you can massively increase the effectiveness of your Outstanding Operations manual without it taking you an eternity to create.

- Make the process visual: a simple flow diagram from Microsoft Word SmartArt makes for a really easy-to-follow visual process.
- Film your work: use tools like CamStudio, GotoMeeting or Camtasia to record your screen and your commentary. That way, you can build an Outstanding Operation while working on the job. All you need to do is to add a running commentary to what you are doing. When you are training a new employee, record that.

- Borrow and reference external content: find videos and articles online that explain a concept and drop those links into your Outstanding Operations manual too.

Start by asking yourself what your core business areas are. These should be the most important steps of your client journey and the most important things you do behind the scenes. At the same time as you write up each Outstanding Operation, identify what one improvement you would like to make to each that would make it run even more efficiently.

By creating your Outstanding Operation for each of these areas and incorporating the one improvement you wanted to make for each, you can produce a massively powerful document in very little time. As they say, "Hard work never killed anyone, but why take the risk." In my Better Future coaching, I get people to do an exercise to help them identify the areas of their business that need an Outstanding Operation. You can find out more about this at www.charliereading.com/BF.

PHENOMENAL PROCESS

The other way to clone yourself is to have what I would call a Phenomenal Process that you lead your clients through. In the last chapter we looked at building a UBS, which is all of your intellectual property put into a manageable process, so that you can teach and explain it easily. This is great for explaining the underlying concepts of what you do, but it doesn't explain how you actually do it.

I recently had the pleasure of meeting three new local marketing agencies to help build our strategy for 2019. I love talking about marketing and meeting three agencies allowed us to get the best-fit company. They all met with us for an initial meeting, which was great; we chatted about our business, what we wanted our marketing to look like, and where they saw the opportunities.

Throughout all of the first meetings, I found myself wondering, *what is the next step?* If I work with them, what does it look like in practical terms? It is fantastic to talk about marketing concepts but, as a business owner, I need to know what is involved. How much time, how many meetings, timeframes, etc. Not one of them explained to me their process and, in every case, I found myself asking what it would actually look like.

Maybe this was a reflection of speaking to more 'creative types,' but I'd say it equally applies to both left-brain thinkers and right-brain thinkers. I can't remember ever having a clearly laid out explanation of the process from any accountants or solicitors we have met either.

As a business owner, the steps of your process are obvious to you. You know your subject like the back of your hand, and you assume that everyone else does too. The reality is that they almost certainly don't. Even people who have used similar services won't know exactly how you will work with them, and people who are using your industry's services for the first time don't stand a chance.

When I first joined the crazy commission-hungry world of City Financial Partners and Biggsy back in 1999, I was told that there was a simple two-step sales process: book the client in for what was imaginatively known as a 'first,' a fact-finding meeting where you needed to find out what you could sell them; and then to book the equally imaginatively named 'second,' which was the sales meeting proper. Pretty straightforward. I knew what it was, but the clients didn't.

Over the years of constantly evolving Efficient Portfolio's business practices, we improved what we did, we embraced financial planning as opposed to just giving financial advice and, therefore, added additional steps to improve the structure.

Our process now looks like this:

FREE FINANCE CALL

A free call with a financial planner to make sure we can help and to identify the best person at Efficient Portfolio to do so.

THE EXPLORATION MEETING

A face-to-face meeting with a financial planner to help you understand how we work, understand where you currently are with your finances and, most importantly, to help give you a clearer understanding of what you want to achieve in the future. This meeting is free of charge.

THE EFFICIENT FINANCIAL PLAN

A bespoke financial plan that gives you clarity on whether you are on track for the financial future you want, analyses your existing financial planning to work out what's good and what's not, and then gives you the approach and strategies to improve it and, ultimately, improve that financial future. This will include strategies for your investments, for your retirement, including pensions, an estate plan so that you can protect the assets for your loved ones, as well as other elements of financial planning. We send this in the post and electronically and charge a flat fee for the plan, but it is covered by a 100% money-back guarantee.

THE PLANNING MEETING

Once you've had a chance to read your Efficient Financial Plan, you have a Planning Meeting with your financial planner. If you have any questions, this meeting ensures they are answered and that you understand everything clearly, so you can make the best decisions to move forwards. The fees for implementing our ideas are all clearly laid out in the plan for you to see.

THE IMPLEMENTATION MEETING
An opportunity for your client relationship manager to guide you through paperwork to implement your financial plan in the most pain-free and efficient way.

THE PROGRESSIVE REVIEW PROGRAMME
An ongoing review service that ensures you keep on top of your finances and continue to make the most of the financial planning opportunities that present themselves, because you need to ensure your planning evolves with your ever-changing life, the legislation and the investment markets. This includes face-to-face meetings with your financial planner, workshops and regular updates.

This process is called The Efficient Wealth Management Process and is clearly explained to all new clients before and during our Exploration Meeting. As a result, our clients clearly know what the process looks like.

By building a Phenomenal Process, you can clearly explain what each client can expect. In addition, you are making the process repeatable, which means you can, over time, clone yourself and get other people to do the same thing. Our clients are told that, regardless of the adviser they see, they will all follow the same process.

As the face of the business, I used to think that people only wanted to see me. Over time, I've realized that isn't the case. If people know that they will be guided through my process regardless of the financial planner, they are happy that they are still getting my expertise, even without me seeing them. In addition, clients also get the same advice, as we manage decisions like investment strategy from the top down.

Finally, through our Outstanding Operations, specifically through my recording of what the ideal Exploration Meeting and Planning Meeting looks and feels like, my financial planners even sound like me. However, I want them to, because I want them to reach the same level I have in a fraction of that time.

Finally, with regard to your Phenomenal Process, it is important that you name each stage. I named our stages years ago, long before I even attended Strategic Coach; they aren't what I would name them now if I was starting fresh. That said, given everything we have built around them, it would be a lot of work to rename them now.

The reason to name them is so that they are unique to you. You cannot get an Efficient Financial Plan from anywhere else other than from Efficient Portfolio. It differentiates us from our competitors. Make sure when you name your process, and the stages within it, the names are based on the benefits people get from using them. Focus on the benefits, not the features.

In order that you can get your time back, you need to clone yourself with repeatable and scalable processes, so I have put together an exercise for you to work through. This can be found in *The Entrepreneurial Happiness Workbook*, that you can download for free from www.charliereading.com/EH.

CHAPTER SUMMARY

- Make your business more scalable, predictable and valuable by building a set of Outstanding Operations so that you have each and every process in the business documented.

- Help many more people while gaining more free time by cloning yourself, getting people to deliver your service as you would, time and again.

CHAPTER 10

DELEGATE YOUR WAY TO SUCCESS!

If you want to grasp your work-life balance by the horns and take back control of your life, there is one major key to your success. If you want the time to spend with the people who are important to you, have the opportunity to do the activities you enjoy the most, and have the flexibility to keep yourself healthy, then you've got to nail this section.

For instance, there is a constant stream of cooking programmes on television. Whether it is Jamie cooking Italian, wannabe chefs cooking for Gregg Wallace and John Torode, or Heston mastering the perfect lemon tart, the culinary shows never stop. One day I remember watching Raymond Blanc, the proud owner of two Michelin stars, preparing some delicate canapés for the show. Standing behind Raymond was another chef. Are far as I could see, the sole responsibility of this man was to take things from the fridge and pass them to Raymond.

What Raymond demonstrated was delegation. Most business owners are poor at delegation, as they are worried that they can do a better job, can do it more quickly than training someone else, and begrudge paying someone to do something they could have done themselves. But Raymond evidently sees the benefit in delegation and was, therefore, able to concentrate on his own task of cooking, which is his talent.

We looked in the last chapter at how to create Outstanding Operations so that you can delegate more effectively. Once you have them in place, you can become better and better at delegating. When I ask members of my team to delegate a part of their role to someone else so that they can spend more time focusing on their own unique talents and abilities, they often find it difficult. They think it is something you are either good at or you are not. They think that I am a naturally good delegator. I am not. Like anything, though, it just took practice.

So many people believe that the geniuses of the modern world were born as naturally gifted people. Whether it be David Beckham, Mozart, the Williams sisters or Bill Gates, it is easy for us to believe that they were born that way. But this simply isn't true. They worked hard to create their talent. Essentially, they put themselves in a position where they could get more purposeful practice than anyone else.

Let's take Mozart, for example. Despite popular misconception, even Mozart was trained, not just talented. His father was a very talented composer, and a very hard task master and, as a result, Mozart just happened to receive excellent training, starting before he was four years old. Also contrary to popular belief, Mozart likely only started composing 'proper' music in his teenage years. His earlier work was essentially reworkings of other music around at the time. Even that shows signs that it could have actually been the work of his father. By the time Mozart became a teenager, he had had more deliberate practice than anyone else around at the time, because by then he had put in a decade's worth of deliberate practice already.

In *Mindset*, Carol Dweck looks at the difference between a 'growth mindset' and a 'fixed mindset.' People who have a fixed mindset believe that you are either naturally good at something, or you aren't. This is a dangerous belief, as it causes you to accept what is, rather than to change it to what you want. A growth mindset, on the other hand, always believes you can get better and better; you just need the right practice at whatever it is you want to improve at.

Going back to my original point, I was not a good delegator, but by reading books I got plenty of deliberate practice. I learned how to delegate, and now I find it very easy. Delegation is not just about getting people who are better than you to do a particular role. It is about giving you the opportunity to get deliberate practice in order to continue to perfect your own abilities.

The key to being successful in business is to find the things that you are a.) really good at, and b.) you really enjoy, and only do those things. Delegate everything else. I do this through regularly using 'the job list delegator exercise.' You may not be able to do so immediately but create a plan so that you can. However, to do that you need to know all the things you currently do, so let's start with that. Look back over the last week, month and year and list the jobs that you have been doing while at work. List everything, from checking your emails to changing the toilet rolls.

This isn't always easy looking backwards; you may need to have this on your desk for the next week or more so you don't miss anything.

Once done, take all of these jobs and put them into one of four boxes:

1. Jobs you love and are great at
2. Jobs you love but aren't that good at
3. Jobs you dislike but you are great at
4. Jobs you don't like, and you aren't that good at

You should now have a list of jobs in each section. You will notice that box 1 contains all the jobs you are great at and you enjoy. This is the stuff that gets you excited in the morning, and the stuff that is at the core of your business, and the likely reason you got into it in the first place. At the other end of the scale, the jobs in box 4 are the jobs you hate and that you really aren't very good at. Maybe you once enjoyed them, and maybe you used to think you were good at them, but now you don't.

Now we move onto the fun bit. Step 3 is to identify ways to delegate all of the items in box 4, and as many in box 3 as possible.

When I first did this, I thought this was a one-off exercise. I went through the list in category 4, and over time,

I delegated every one of those roles. Then I realized I needed to start to delegate the items listed in boxes 2 and 3 too. Some I had to retain, because of the regulatory nature of our business, but I got rid of most. When I came back to this exercise again a few years later, I didn't think there was anything left I could delegate, but guess what, there was loads because what happens is that over time, you break jobs down into more granular parts.

For example, I initially had 'running the business' as one of my tasks. Over time, that has been broken down into many smaller parts, which allows me to delegate more and more of that role. As a result, I now go through this exercise once a year. Each time I go into it thinking, "I just cannot delegate any more of my roles out," and each year I identify significant amounts of each role that I can delegate. What this means is that over time I am refining down my element and asking other people to do all but those elements; people that in the most part are better at them than me.

I'd encourage you to do the same, and repeat this exercise on an annual basis. Do you think that when Raymond Blanc was originally recruiting at the start of launching Le Manoir aux Quat'Saisons, he thought he needed a 'fridge-assistant?' Of course not! But over time he realized that even stepping away from his workstation reduced the amount of time he spent doing his element, and so that's when he recruited him.

As I've already said, not only does having a 'fridge assistant' allow you to spend more time doing what you do best, to maximize its impact and allow you to perfect that even more by doing it more than anyone else, it is also the key to claiming back your work-life balance. It is the one thing that allows your business to continue to grow, without it being at your own expense.

OUTSOURCED EFFICIENCY

The wonderful thing about the job list delegator exercise is that, the more I do it, the more profitable we become as a business. I am left to do the things I am best at, and others are allowed to do the bits that they are better at than me. It makes sense that we can all do more of those roles and make more money. However, I appreciate that when you first do this, you may not immediately have sufficient team members to delegate all roles. Someone once said to me that you should employ the next person when you think you can fill 50% of their time, as you'll soon find things to fill the rest once they are onboard.

That said, I appreciate that you may have financial constraints that stop you from just going out and hiring more people, or logistical constraints that means you cannot recruit the right people quickly. The wonderful thing today is that there is likely to be a technological solution that might fit the bill. Over the years, we have outsourced some of our work to other companies in the UK, but also to people working in Argentina, the Philippines and India, to name just a few. Clearly certain activities need to be done by people who are based in your home country, but many do not. You can have a virtual assistant who takes care of most of your life without even having an employment contract.

OUTSOURCED INBOX

Most business owners, and now employees too, are slaves to their inbox. We all know we look at our phones too much but looking at your business inbox in the evening is just wrong. In fact, I'll go further than that: looking at your business inbox, as the business owner, is always wrong.

In this day and age, there is so much spam and marketing nonsense that finds its way into our inbox that we are bogged down by it. On the flip side, some people just ignore it, and when they look at their phone they have 3,587 emails still in their inbox, and then they wonder why they miss things. Others spend their lives fighting a losing battle of whether they should reply to this email now or later.

I almost never look at my inbox. I haven't for over eight years now. I know what you are thinking: boy, there must be a lot of emails in there by now. Clearly, I could not run a successful business if someone and something wasn't doing this on my behalf. Here are the secrets to my success.

STEP 1: Unsubscribe to anything you don't look at almost every time. Yes, you might miss an offer for 10% off your next pair of jeans, but the time and stress you'll save in going through deleting 100 emails a day will more than compensate, I promise.

STEP 2: Use 'Rules' to divert certain messages from certain people into specific folders. I have a folder called 'Team' that automatically receives any emails from anyone in my team. I have another that is linked to our investment managers, so that I don't miss their communications. Minimize the amount of time it takes to organize your emails by using technology wherever possible.

STEP 3: Set up multiple email addresses. For example, I have news@efficientportfolio.co.uk. Anything that sounds like a newsletter will be subscribed to this email address. That way, I can set up another rule to divert those emails automatically into a 'News' folder.

STEP 4: Only your personal assistant or your virtual assistant gets to look at your inbox. If you don't have a PA or a VA, reread the last section and see what might be feasible for you. You'll be amazed at how little it will cost you.

STEP 5: Create a 'Focus' folder and a 'Buffer' folder and draw out clear instructions as to what types of emails go into each. Also draw out clear instructions as to what can be delegated and to whom. This is a good example of an Outstanding

Operation. Buffer emails are anything that isn't urgent, that if you don't read for two weeks, it won't hurt. Tell your PA/VA to check your email three times a day and, at each point, ask them to delegate to a team member, as per your instructions, or delete or file the rest in the relevant folder. Aim for no more than three focused emails a day from your PA/VA.

STEP 6: Check your Focus and Team emails three times a day. This allows you to focus on what's important for the rest of the day. At a set time, no more than once a week, review your news and buffer folders. Be ruthless at clearing stuff out quickly. Unsubscribe from anything that isn't important, as it will save you and your PA/VA time later. You may even want to adopt using a platform such as Slack to communicate with your team to prevent too many emails from this front.

STEP 7: Sit back and watch the magic happen; you've just got a whole chunk of your life back. Your daily emails will drop from 100 to the three you see in 'Focus,' plus any communications with your team.

For many people, this one seemingly simple thing can be a complete game changer.

DELEGATION SUCCESS STRATEGIES

Delegating aspects of your business can be a scary thing. Initially I found it very difficult, but over time, I have gotten much better at it. It comes back to 'practice, practice, practice.' It is difficult to pass over a job that you know you can do to someone who you aren't yet sure can do it quite as well. It is a psychological barrier that you need to get over, but there are some ways to make it easier.

First, this is a tricky one, but you have to accept that they are going to make some mistakes at some point. That said, so do you. No one is perfect; it is easy to justify our own mistakes because we can see the other factors involved. Even if they make a mistake more often than you, the importance of you giving up these tasks is so great that this is a price worth paying.

Second, create amazing processes or Outstanding Operations that are full of checklists to ensure mistakes are minimal.

Third, create a decision-making process for the team. Ours at Efficient Portfolio is:

1. Is it legal?
2. Is it compliant and ethical?
3. Does it keep Efficient Portfolio viable to deliver what we do best?
4. Is it in the client's best interests?
5. Is it in the team's best interests?

If your team follow this process, they should arrive at the right decision. Why not create one for your company?

In addition to identifying the aspects of your overall role that you can delegate, revisit this when you create your task list for the week ahead. More about this concept later on, but when you look down your to-do list each day/week, first think about which of those roles you could delegate. If you can delegate them, ensure that you create an Outstanding Operation for the role so that you never have to do it again.

Delegating as much of your boxes 2, 3 and 4 roles as possible will allow you to expand beyond your wildest dreams and will mean that you have far more free time than you've ever had before. Over time, your box 1 roles will also probably change and, by repeating the delegation exercise time and again, you can constantly ensure that you are doing the best role for yourself and your business.

If you keep rinsing and repeating this exercise over the years, it will gradually transform your business. If you want freedom, master delegation!

CHAPTER SUMMARY

- If you truly want to get more of your time back, you need to identify better ways to delegate. As a business owner, you need to learn to become an expert delegator.

- Easily upscale your business and achieve more without taking on another employed person by using outsourced solutions.

- Give yourself more freedom by delegating your inbox.

CHAPTER 11

ENERGY ABOUND

People often ask me, "Where do you get your energy from?" In addition to running a number of businesses, taking at least 12 weeks of holiday a year with the family and doing the school run a couple times a week, I have just completed Ironman Italy, which involved a 2.4 mile swim, 112 mile bike ride and a 26.2 mile run.

Because a significant part of my role at Efficient Portfolio is finding new clients for the financial planners, I do end up doing a number of breakfast and evening seminars. This makes family time and training difficult, but both are important enough to make sure they happen.

A typical week for me is to be up at 5.30 every day. I swim roughly three kilometres Monday and Friday morning, I run roughly five miles Tuesday and Thursday morning, and I cycle 50–80 miles Friday afternoon or Saturday morning. All that takes a lot of time. In addition, at work I need to be full of energy because when you are managing a team, presenting from the stage or holding a client meeting, my three main roles in the business, I need to have energy. That's because, in every instance, clients feed off my energy. If I am lacklustre, the results will also reflect that.

When I'm presenting at our Breakthrough Business Breakfast at 7am, running five miles at lunchtime, and then presenting again at our Leaving a Legacy Seminar until 8pm, I am usually tired by bedtime. That said, by morning I am in the pool swimming three kilometres again because I have the energy to do so.

It wasn't, however, always like this. Not so many years ago, I was into playing squash. It was the one thing that kept my excess weight from getting even worse. Typically, I played in the evening, but it was tricky organizing some of the league games. Inevitably, occasionally I would suggest that we play before work, if it was the only way we could get the game in before the end of the month.

The funny thing was that, my squash, normally a reasonable level, was appalling at this time of the morning. I remember losing matches and missing shots that would have been easy wins in the evening.

During these early morning games, which were being played at 7.30am, my coordination was off, I tired more easily and my strategic play was dreadful. Interestingly, for some of my opponents, they were equally as bad. If you want to run a healthy business, you need to run a healthy body and also have a healthy team around you. If you want to have an energized business, you need to be an energized person and have an energized team. If you want to have a happy team, you need to be a happy leader.

The question you are probably asking though is, what changed? Why, just a few years ago, when I was obviously younger than I am now, did I have less energy than I have today? As I told you in my story, it all started at Unleash the Power Within. Had I continued making the same decisions as I had at the time of that event, I might be telling a very different story now.

What you need is leverage to make a significant change. As Tony Robbins says, if you asked a smoker wanting to give up smoking tomorrow, they'd tell you it was difficult and maybe impossible for them to achieve. If you then put a gun to their head and asked them the same question, suddenly it becomes a lot easier. So, it is all about leverage! If it is important enough you will do it; the question is, how do you make it important, how do you give yourself the leverage?

In order that you can create the leverage to ensure you do take your health seriously and achieve the results you know you want and need, I have put together an exercise for you to work through. This can be found in *The Entrepreneurial Happiness Workbook*, that you can download for free from www.charliereading.com/EH.

THE B.E.T.T.E.R. BODY SYSTEM

The B.E.T.T.E.R. Body System stands for: Blood, Energy, Toxins, Two-week detox, Exercise and Rules, so let me explain more.

BLOOD

Many of the toxins we routinely put into our body as a result of today's modern lifestyle cause our blood to become more acidic. Acidic blood is less efficient at supplying our cells with the nutrients they need, as it becomes gloopy, which is not a good consistency for blood. Things that cause this are caffeine, alcohol, dairy products, gluten and sugar. If you want to create more energy, you need to eliminate these from your diet or at least drastically reduce them.

When I quit caffeine, I started getting thumping headaches. But after about two weeks, I suddenly realized I felt so much better than I ever had before, particularly in the mornings. I started being able to happily rise earlier and exercise earlier. Before I eradicated caffeine, I only drank about two coffees a day, but it turns out there was an underlying level in my system that was affecting me.

One way you can speed up the recovery of your blood is by adding some wheatgrass to your morning drink. Furthermore, when I had a couple of years off this, I noticed I started succumbing to bugs like colds again, which since reintroducing frozen wheatgrass to my morning, I have not had since.

An even simpler way to help deacidify your blood is to add a slice of lemon to your water. Have a hot water and lemon as your first hot drink of the day, too. Bizarre as it sounds, as lemons are obviously acidic, the effect that this has on your blood is to deacidify. It's a really easy way to cleanse your blood.

ENERGY

You need to live on a diet that boosts your energy. Sugar and white, starchy carbohydrates may initially feel like they are giving you energy, but they are like putting paper on the fire. It burns like crazy for a few minutes and then disappears in a flash! That's why after eating a big bowl of pasta or a sandwich at lunchtime, you feel like you need an afternoon nap, and you are starving long before dinner time. They cause your blood sugar to spike and then crash.

The way to eat for sustainable energy is to eat an 80% natural diet, thinking about food combinations and correcting your omega balance. Eating the right food to generate energy is about providing your body with the nutrients it needs in a form it can digest. As a result, I try to eat a diet of 80% natural food; that is, 80% of what I eat is made up of fruit and vegetables and not too much fruit either, as it contains a lot of sugar!

After the Industrial Revolution, humans started to consume much greater levels of Omega-6 through the consumption of vegetable oils and cereals, and our Omega-6 to Omega-3 ratio started to shift much more heavily towards Omega-6. During the 20th century, vegetable oil and cereal consumption again rose dramatically, and it is estimated that most people today consume a diet with an Omega-6 to Omega-3 ratio of between 10:1 and 20:1, with some people reaching as high a ratio as 25:1. It should be about 1:1! Eat plenty of fish and vegetables and stay away from processed foods, and you should see that start to change. This is also one of the leading causes of heart attacks and strokes, as a high Omega 6:3 balance causes inflammation in the body.

TOXINS

Toxins are everywhere in our daily life. They build up in our system and are known to significantly increase the likelihood of diseases like Alzheimer's and cancer. I want to stack the odds in my favour, so my family and I try, whenever possible, to select aluminium-free deodorants, paraben-free plastics and paraben-free cosmetics. I dare say, with the benefit of hindsight some of these decisions will have proved to be a waste of time but, if just one was worthwhile, it will have been worth the effort. After all, it may be the difference between living out my own dream retirement or not!

One of the best ways to reduce toxins in your body, to feel better and to eat less, is to drink sufficient water. Most people are in a permanent state of dehydration, and this encourages them to eat more, as the sensations are similar. I drink between two and three litres of water every day. I'd recommend that you find an online water calculator and work out how much you should be drinking, then stick to it. What gets measured gets done!

TWO-WEEK DETOX

When I left Unleash the Power Within, Tony Robbins set us a challenge. It was to complete a two-week detox based on the principles above. Tony challenged me that if I felt good after two weeks, I should then, in some format, stick to it as closely as possible. If you would like to see my version of that detox, you can download it from www.efficientportfolio.co.uk/detox. You can do anything for two weeks. Just try it, and if you feel better at the end of two weeks, hopefully with the leverage you've created for yourself, you'll stick to some or all of it.

EXERCISE

It is important that you not only get enough exercise, but that you get a variety. If you want to be as healthy as you can be, you should be doing aerobic exercise where you can easily breathe throughout, like golf or cycling, and anaerobic exercise, where you cannot breathe so easily, like running or squash.

You should also do exercises that cause you to stretch, like Pilates or yoga, and exercises that cause you to strengthen your muscles, like lifting weights and resistance training. If you can create an exercise plan that includes all of these, you could be in the best shape possible for your future.

We think that keeping fit is all about keeping our body in good shape, but it is also about our mind. Research shows that our cognitive activity is improved after exercise. Not only do we feel healthier from exercise, feel happier from the endorphins it produces, but it also helps us think better too. Amazing. As a result, I do a lot of my thinking while exercising. When Steve Jobs wanted to think or discuss a difficult subject, he would do so while going for a walk. There is something about moving that helps the brain work. When I am planning a book, preparing for a talk or brainstorming a problem at work, I realize now I do it best while running or cycling. So not only am I getting fitter, I am thinking better at the same time. That sounds like a win-win situation to me.

RULES

If you want to make lasting changes, the key is to make some rules for yourself. The two-week detox may seem complicated, but actually over time I've made it pretty simple to live by. I am a good wine and meat lover, so I am probably never going to give up either entirely. I love a nice coffee and life without the dairy-gluten combination of a delicious pizza would, in my opinion, be a dull affair. I enjoy all of these things, but it's the rules I create for myself that keep me living a healthy life. To give you a guide, here they are:

1. Five days a week I stick to a vegan diet plus fish. I don't drink alcohol, or consume refined sugar, caffeine or gluten at home or work.
2. I do two swims, two runs and two rides.

They are simple, and they give me flexibility. You only get one body, so look after it.

A HAPPY PERSPECTIVE

As a business owner, there is always bad news. There is bad news in the press, there is that client who turns their back on you, or the prospect who refuses to take your advice. If you don't have thick skin, these can all get you down. If you read too much bad news, it can paralyze you into not taking action, and this stops you improving as a business. A worried and stressed business owner or partner does not make a good leader, as that fear translates across your team.

One thing that can easily get the most resilient entrepreneur down is bad news, so let's talk about kicking the constant news habit of today's society. After all, NEWS does stand for negative events world service. In today's world of 24/7 news, it is easy to get caught up in watching the news three times a day, reading the paper and catching up online. Many would say that this is allowing you to be informed and up to date with today's important stories, and I can appreciate that argument, but does it make you happy? Only a small fraction of all news that you consume is good news. Is that because good things don't happen? Of course not, good things happen all the time, but bad news makes good news, as they say.

I would argue that consuming this level of news, particularly when you are unlikely to do anything about it, only serves the purpose of draining your happiness. When you are working, you need to keep up with what is relevant to your field. If you are a banker, you need to read the *Financial Times* as part of your job. I need to know financial services news so that I can give the best advice to my clients. But I don't need to hear doom and gloom all day, every day. Since I started to take this approach about three years ago,

I know nearly as much as I did beforehand (and on the topics important to me, I know even more), but I am also far happier. Most of the bad news will never happen anyway. How many times have you heard an economist talking doom and gloom about the year ahead? As they say, economists have predicted 12 of the last three recessions! Eventually they are right, but that is more by luck than judgement.

You can be a pessimist, and possibly be right but miserable; or you can be an optimist, and possibly be right but be happy. I know which I prefer.

In *The Rational Optimist*, Matt Ridley discusses the gap between reality and our perceptions. When surveyed, most people felt that murder rates were on the rise, due to the increased publicity of each death. But when you look at the reality of the situation (see Ridley's chart), you realize that compared to 700 years ago, murders are almost non-existent today. It's all about perception.

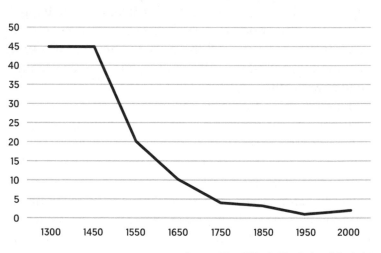

HOMICIDE RATES IN EUROPE

Source: Matt Ridley's *The Rational Optimist*

Initially, when taking the approach of not consuming as much news, you think you might miss something important. You won't. That guilt is soon replaced with a feeling of contentment. How many people go to sleep where the last thing they have watched is about a war-torn part of the world on the 10 o'clock news, and then the first thing they watch over their bowl of cereal is the very same topic? Most of the time, nothing has changed.

In today's world, it is also very easy to set up a stream of specific news that is important to you. For example, I set up a Twitter feed that provides me with a constant stream of financial services news. I can look anytime I want, but I am not bombarded with it when I don't, like on my Free Days® (more on that in a bit). You can look at specific publications, whether that be online or through traditional media. That way you can consume news as and when you want to without constantly infecting your brain with global misery.

THE GIVER OF GRATITUDE

It is impossible to feel anger when you are feeling grateful. By focusing on the things in life you are grateful for each day, you can take a step closer to entrepreneurial happiness. Whether you do this as part of writing a journal each morning, a Facebook group of like-minded people, using an app like 'Grateful' or in your head while you are exercising or meditating, make sure you do. It is a wonderful gift to the soul.

In my Better Future coaching, I get people to do exercises called 'the best things' and 'the gratitude giver' to help them become happier and more positive. You can find out more about this at www.charliereading.com/BF.

THE SIX HUMAN NEEDS

One of the principles we spent time focusing on at Unleash the Power Within is the 'six human needs.' Based on 'Maslow's human needs,' Tony Robbins enhanced and improved this to create his own version. Let's look at them through a business owner's eyes.

1. CERTAINTY

In order to be happy, we need certainty in our life. We need to know our business is safe for the future and that we have sufficient income to pay our bills. If we don't have certainty in our business and personal life, we will be distinctly unhappy, as it will cause huge levels of stress.

2. UNCERTAINTY/VARIETY

We also need life to be different or uncertain. If you do the same thing in your business day in day out, you will become bored. You need to create variety in your life, otherwise you will lose your motivation to do what you do.

3. SIGNIFICANCE

We all need to feel significance; the question is just how much. A business owner with a team around them often feels significant, as they have a team of people trying to help them achieve their goals. That said, if you don't have a team, or your team are not helping you as much as they should, a lack of significance will start to get you down. This is no more obvious than when business owners get together socially, and they are all trying to show that they are the most significant.

4. CONNECTION/LOVE

In life, we all need connection to others. In your personal life, hopefully you get as far as love, but in business you need to be spending your time with people you like. Whether that be your clients or your team, if you are not spending your time around people you want to be with, you will be an unhappy entrepreneur.

Those four human needs are your core needs. Everyone needs these addressed if they want to be happy; however, to be truly happy, you also need to satisfy the final two human needs.

5. GROWTH

If you aren't growing, you are dying. For a business owner, if you are not getting better, you are falling behind. If your business isn't continually innovating, you are losing ground on the competition. If you are not improving as a person, you too are losing ground.

6. CONTRIBUTION

Finally, to be truly happy, you need to feel that you are making a contribution. Whether that is by improving the lives of your clients, your team or the charitable work that comes out of your company, it is up to you.

Each person has differing demands in each area. You will also have one or two areas that are most important to you, that is, unless one is not being satisfied at all. For example, perhaps 'significance' is your most important human need; however, if suddenly you lose your certainty because of a recession, that will temporarily jump to the top of the pile until you get enough 'Certainty' for you to feel comfortable again. Let's take a look at this from your perspective.

To help you identify how well you are meeting each need and what you can do to improve each area, I have put together an exercise for you to work through. This can be found in *The Entrepreneurial Happiness Workbook*, that you can download for free from www.charliereading.com/EH.

If you want to be truly happy, then you need to ensure that all of your six human needs are met, not just to their minimum level, but to your desired level. By looking at this each year, I find it allows me to see where my life is not quite delivering everything I want and need. I find it is a really good exercise to then allow me to highlight what I can change to make it even better. It is also a really good exercise to go through with your loved ones, as it helps you see how you could help them change their lives to make them even happier.

CHAPTER SUMMARY

- In order to be the best business leader, you need to live a life that generates more energy and that comes with taking your health seriously.

- If you want to have a healthy business, you need to have a healthy business owner and healthy team.

- The best way to achieve this is to create massive leverage; a hugely compelling reason why you must become the healthiest you can be.

- Take a step towards a healthier future by following The B.E.T.T.E.R. Body System.

- To truly embrace entrepreneurial happiness, you need to be content and happy in yourself. You can achieve this by focusing on the things you are grateful for.

- Better understand what makes you happy by understanding the six human needs.

CHAPTER 12

A LIFE LESS ORDINARY

Have you ever found that time distorts our memories?

Time distorts reality. Often what seemed brilliant years ago doesn't appear so today. Also, what seemed huge when you were younger seems so small now. If you want to master Entrepreneurial Happiness, you need to master your 'time.' There have been many great business books written on time management, which all seem to recount some good principles, but you need to read a lot on the topic to really grasp the concept as a whole.

They say that if you want something done, you should ask a busy person. This is so true. Those achievers seem to get so much more done than anyone else, and yet, as far as I am aware, we all only have 24 hours in the day to work with. How do they do it? People often ask me, where do I find the time for it all? After all, I take 12 weeks holiday a year with my family, I run three companies, I've written three books in the last four years, I've got my handicap in golf down to 12 and I have been training for an Ironman. It's all about time management and delegation. So let's look a little more deeply at time.

RIPPED GROWTH ENERGIZER

What are my roles in life? First, and most importantly, I am a husband and a dad. I need to keep myself in great shape and so that's another. In my business life I am primarily a business owner. I am then a financial planner and also a marketeer. That is three personal roles and three business roles. I have clearly defined what each is and, even better, they each have a name. Want to know what they are? I admit they are somewhat cringeworthy, but when I see them, I know exactly what they sum up. Here goes me bearing my soul.

PERSONAL

Dad	Super dad
Husband	Dream husband
Health	Ripped growth energizer *(slight blush)*

BUSINESS

Business owner	Business growth specialist
Financial planner	Builder of dreams
Marketeer	Marketing money magnet *(slight cringe)*

These have been the names of my three roles for roughly the last eight years. When I build my goals, I build them for each of these roles. Every quarter, month and even week I set out goals that are going to deliver my one-year and three-year goals for each of these roles. The reason this is so important is that, for each of my small weekly goals, I know that they are doing two things. First, I know that they are a step towards my bigger goals, but second, they are a part of me living that role and why they are important.

For example, I hate checking another person's work. It is my least favourite activity at work, but sometimes that is what I have to do. That said, if it is part of me delivering amazing financial planning to a client, and I know it is part of me being 'the builder of dreams,' I am more excited to get it done. I cannot push it to the back burner, because that would be me failing in that role. It is my leverage for every element of what I do.

To help you build better and more compelling goals I have put together an exercise for you to work through. This can be found in *The Entrepreneurial Happiness Workbook*, which you can download for free from www.charliereading.com/EH.

NE TIME

When listing my business roles, you'll notice that I said that when it came to my business life, I said I was a business owner first and a financial planner second. I absolutely believe this has to be the case. If I want to be a financial planner first, I need to be employed or pay for an MD to run Efficient Portfolio. This is a mistake that many small business owners make. If you run your own business, you have to be a business owner first, and then your professional career is your second role. That means you need to read more on running a business than you do on being a professional.

If you get this bit wrong, you will likely fail or, at minimum, have a massively stressful business existence. If you only want to be your professional role, then you need someone else to be taking care of running the business bit, because it is massively important. What good are your professional skills if your business fails?

I am sure you are a great accountant, land agent, solicitor, whatever you are, but are you a great business owner? If you aren't, given it is your most important business role, what can you do about it? What books can you read to improve the way you see and run your business? Throughout this book I have given you many book recommendations, but later in this book I provide you with my top business books to read, so that would be a great place to start.

Think about booking yourself on a course to learn more about the management of your business and time.

When it comes to reading, I have read over 150 business and personal development books in the last few years, but where do I find the time? As a dyslexic person I am a hopelessly slow reader, too, which compounds the problem; except it doesn't, because I read these books in NE time. NE stands for 'No Extra' time.

'NE time' is time that you were spending doing something else but where you can add in an extra activity, to buy yourself double the amount of time. The simplest example I can give you of this is how I read these books or, more accurately, listened to these books. When I discovered audiobooks it was a revelation, because suddenly I could consume books at the speed that everyone else does; but not only that, I could do so when I was doing other things. When I am in the car, on the bike or even running, I listen to books.

I used to just listen to one book at a time, but I've realized that different books work for me during different activities. For running, I need personal development or fitness. For driving and cycling, I like business and marketing books, and for holidays I like biographies, with the odd drop of fiction thrown in.

I have also discovered another way to use audiobooks to enhance my NE time. I now listen to different books at different speeds, for two reasons. First, some books, like business books, I need a little more thinking time, so I'll listen to them at 1.5x speed. I know that will sound fast to you initially, but the brain soon adapts to that. Occasionally, for a certain book I'll need to go back down to 1x speed, but it's rare now. When I am on a biography, where I don't need so much thinking time and the attention to detail, I'll up it to 2x speed. At this speed I am reading twice as many books as I used to. Even at 1.5x, I am reading four books in the time it previously took to read three. The second reason I listen to books at different speeds is that I have found that some books work better at different speeds.

NE time doesn't just apply to listening to books, however. It can be applied to exercise, too. So, how can you multitask your day? Caryl says that I cannot multitask, and in many ways she is right, but when it comes to listening to audiobooks, she is definitely wrong. I can absorb books while doing other things. Likewise, if I need to watch a webinar, I'll be thinking can I do this while sat on the exercise bike or treadmill? Even when you are walking around between meetings, there is always NE time. For example, walking down the escalators in the underground or taking the stairs in the office rather than the lift; not only do you possibly get to your destination faster, you've just squeezed some more exercise into your busy day, without giving it any time! Result. If one of the girls has a birthday party they need taking to, I will go for a run or a cycle while I wait. Don't just hang around reading the newspaper or looking at your phone; see it as an opportunity to fit in something important. We waste a lot more time than we realize, and NE time forces you to revaluate that. What can you do during your day in NE time? If you think hard, I bet you can cram in a whole load more activities without it costing you any more time. Get creative.

THE TIME SYSTEM

I learned to split my time up into three types of days – Free Days®, Focus Days® and Buffer Days®.

On my Focus Days®, I only do the things that make us profitable. I only do these activities, nothing else, because it is better for me, my team and my clients that I work with this structure. In the early days this was difficult, but I would be allowed to do 80% focus activities and 20% buffer.

At the time, my focus activities were:

1. Seeing and speaking to clients
2. Working on improving our business
3. Working with and organizing my team

As the business has evolved, these too have evolved and are now:

1. Seeing to our top clients
2. Managing our business
3. Marketing our business
4. Thinking

On my Focus Days®, I am only allowed to do these activities because this ensures that I maximize my time at work into only doing the parts of the job that I am best at.

Don't get me wrong: I need to do other tasks during a week, so these are reserved for my Buffer Days®. On a Buffer Day®, I do anything else that is required, and if any focus activity happens too, then all the better. But it is these Buffer Days® that allow me to be organized and effective on my Focus Days®. Over time, however, I have delegated more and more of the buffer activities, which means I can now keep that to around half per week.

Finally, I have my Free Days®, where from midnight through to midnight I do not look at, engage in or think about work. This includes not checking emails. It does the mind good to have a break from a particular subject, and I am much better on my Focus Days® as a result of these rules.

You too can apply this principle to your life by first determining what activities fall into the focus category for you. For example, it may be that creating accounts is one of Your Key Roles because not only are you really good at it, you also enjoy it. If it is, that should be one of your focus activities. Remember though, these activities should be the things that you are best at, enjoy, and that make the company money. If you go back to the job list delegator exercise, these should ideally be the things in box 1.

The next step is to build 'The Happy Week.' For me, Mondays are about being in the office with my team, ensuring they are set for the week. This is a Focus Day® for me as I am managing the business. It is also dedicated to organizing myself, so that I can delegate things to my team and implement important priorities for the week. These have become my team Focus Days®.

Tuesdays are about seeing and speaking to clients in our Rutland office and are my Rutland client Focus Days®. Wednesdays are my London client Focus Days®. Thursdays are then left as my marketing Focus Days®.

My Buffer Day® is a Friday, when I do anything else that needs doing. I expect to have this sufficiently well organized by the team so that it is all done by lunchtime, as Friday afternoon is my time for either cycling or golf.

Saturday and Sunday are my Free Days®, where family gets my undivided attention. I am lucky enough to be able to say that I could count on one hand the number of weekends I have worked in recent years, other than when I attend a course or conference that happens to fall on those days, which is also rare now too.

By building The Happy Week, I have built certainty into my week as a matter of course. I know and my team knows where I am likely to be on any one day. They know when to book certain meetings, and I know that I have the certainty of a routine. Clients also know where I am likely to be and when, which gives them certainty too. It also means that I still get variety, as my Free Days® are exactly that. They aren't invaded by work and can be spent with my family.

I would encourage you to think about how you can use these strategies to build The Happy Week. Don't get me wrong; this didn't happen overnight, it took time. It has continued to evolve, but if you don't start, you'll never get to this point. That's why you need to make a start now, and then revisit this again each year, to make sure you are sticking to it.

This allows you to be far more consistent, and that allows you to plan even further. You will remember that from the last chapter that I need to fit in two runs, two swims, and one long or two shorter bike sessions. With a consistent work week, I could do this much more easily. If you can bring simplicity to your week, you will achieve so much more.

By building The Happy Week for work, play and health, you will achieve so much more than most people. Research shows that we perform better in the morning than the afternoon, so also think about which activities are best done during the day. I will try and have client meetings when I need to be on my a-game in the morning, as I know we function better then than in the afternoon. In my Better Future coaching, I get people to do an exercise called The Happy Week worksheet to help them design their perfect week from a work, personal and health perspective. You can find out more about this at www.charliereading.com/BF.

Brian Tracy says that "Every hour spent in preparation saves ten hours in implementation." Not only does planning save you time, but it is also more inherently rewarding, as you achieve increased productivity and, ultimately, have more time for yourself, and that leads me onto the next section nicely.

FAILING TO PLAN = PLANNING TO FAIL

When I tried to master riding a bike with no hands as a child, I had looked down at the road and the bike. These are the obstacles, not where I actually want to go. With this knowledge, I realized I needed a different approach. I needed to focus on where I wanted to go. I also realized that with 'practice, practice, practice,' I could achieve anything I wanted to.

As a result, I repeatedly tried cycling with no hands when out on my own, every time focusing on the horizon ahead of me. Focusing on the prize or the goal as it were. And guess what happened. I mastered it, and I mastered it quickly. By aiming at the goal ahead of me with laser-like focus, I was able to hit it. If you want to achieve what is important to you, you too need to have laser-like focus on those goals. It's all very easy to write goals out and then forget about them. That doesn't ensure you hit them, though. Constantly reminding yourself of what those goals are is more difficult, but this is what is needed if you want to achieve them.

What you can achieve distorts over time. We overestimate what we can achieve in a short period of time, but we massively underestimate what we can achieve in a longer period of time. When I look back on the goals I was writing ten years ago, they seem a lifetime ago. What I wanted to achieve in ten years has easily been surpassed, but each quarter the goals I set seemed like a stretch, and I didn't always achieve them.

That is why your cornerstone for a more successful future is great goal setting and management. I've heard it said that, "Losers have goals, winners have systems,"[3] and this is so right. While just writing down the goal is better than nothing, clearly you need a better strategy if you really want to achieve them. That is where 'the life planner' comes in. This is a document that I have built up over the years to help me on a day-to-day basis to ensure I hit my bigger goals.

If you want to create an amazing future, you need to have some big lifetime goals, but you also need to have shorter-term goals that will get you there. Ninety days, or one quarter of the year, is a great time frame to build your goals around, as you can keep momentum and focus relatively easy over this duration; however, after 90 days, you will start to lose energy. That's why every 90 days you need to revisit those goals and reenergize yourself for the next quarter. Ninety days is also 1% of 25 years, so each quarter needs to be a 1% step towards your lifetime goals.

The secret to having a great system is not just to have lifetime goals and 90-day goals, but also to have several stops in-between. Starting with your lifetime goals is fantastic, but you then need to work backwards. In order to hit your lifetime goals, ask what you need to achieve in the next three years to be on track. In order to do these, what do you need to do this year? In order to achieve this year's goals, what do you need to achieve this quarter? In order to achieve these quarterly goals, what do you need to do this month, and for these monthly goals, what do you have to do this week? Oh, and by the way, you need these for each of your roles.

This sounds like a lot of work, and it is if you don't have a system. That's why I want to share with you 'the limitless life planner,' the secret to my success. It obviously requires more work at the start but, once created, you can build on it. Rather than duplicate your efforts for this, and instead of giving you an exercise table, I'd rather you download the limitless life planner from www.charliereading.com/LLP. Once you have it, watch the explanation video of how to use it and then book half a day in your diary to complete the goals tab.

Not only is the limitless life planner a great tool for writing out your goals, it ensures that you're working through a 'to-do list,' which you should refer to several times a day. The more you can see those goals, the more likely you are to achieve them. You will notice that on the 'Time' tab section of the explanation video, I say your to-do list should also display your quarterly and monthly goals.

That way, you can continually be reminded of what they are. Your four to six most important tasks are also there, staring you in the face each day. By having that constant reminder, you will achieve so much more.

One of the other benefits of the limitless life planner is that it frees up your working memory. As a business owner, you have loads of jobs, ideas and thoughts bouncing around in your head. Things you must remember to do, things you must remember to talk to your team about, and all this would ordinarily clog up your working memory. Not the working memory on your computer, but in your head. This causes unnecessary stress, as you are constantly worried about getting everything done, or that you've missed something.

On a computer, you have a hard disk and you have working memory called Random Access Memory, known as RAM. The hard disk is where everything is stored, and the RAM is where the programs that you are currently working on sit. Have you noticed that as you open more programs, your computer starts to run more slowly? That is because your RAM is being clogged up with too many processes. It has too many things to think about and, as a result, it runs less efficiently. You can speed it up again by closing down some of those programs that you aren't currently using. You brain works the same way. The more things you have whirring around in your brain, the more worried and the less focused you will be. That is why you too need a hard disk, and that is the life planner.

By using the limitless life planner effectively, each time you have an idea or remember something that needs doing, you note it down, knowing that at the right time you can come back to it, regardless of when you think of it. You can park it on your hard disk, the life planner, and then forget about it until it is the right time to address it.

This will ensure you achieve so much more both because you'll never forget anything, and because you are free to focus your attention on what is important in that moment.

3.   Source: https://tinyurl.com/wsbdb6p.

CHAPTER SUMMARY

- Build goals that are more in line with your life's objectives by defining Your Key Roles in your business and personal lives.

- Achieve more in less time by identifying ways to achieve two goals at once.

- Gain a better work-life balance by implementing a time system and constructing The Happy Week.

- Create a goal delivery system that ensures you consistently hit your targets using the limitless life planner.

THE E.P.I.C. BUSINESS BLUEPRINT

**THE 4-STEP GUIDE TO MAKING MORE
TIME IN YOUR BUSINESS LIFE.**

E   End Game

P   Plan

I   Innovate

C   Culture

CHAPTER 13

INNOVATE WITH ENERGI

To truly generate entrepreneurial happiness, the time you spend at work has got to be fun and fulfilling. This comes from a number of areas, one of which is to delegate everything you are either not very good at or you don't enjoy, in the way we looked at in Chapter 10. A wise man once said, "If you are not growing, you're dying," and that applies to your business. As we saw with the six human needs, as individuals we need to feel like we are growing or getting better in order to be genuinely happy. As an entrepreneur, the same applies in your business life. If you don't feel that your business is getting better than it was yesterday, you will never be happy at work.

For instance, Tony Robbins talks about the concept of the business life cycle, which is comparable to the life cycle of a person. At the beginning of your business' life, after its birth, the business is like a toddler. It doesn't really give you anything back, just some grief and the pride of ownership. It is a race for survival, and it needs 100% of your attention. It crashes around from one thing to another and causes as much chaos as it solves. The company is learning to walk.

As the company grows, money is tight, and it is very much a hand-to-mouth business. Cash flow is the biggest restraining factor. That said, your people and your brand are growing. Your business is learning to run.

As a teenager, cash flow is less of a problem because the business is flying high, and you think you're a genius. Almost everything you touch turns to gold. Your business is making progress, and you're making good sales but not necessarily great profits. One of the biggest problems, though, is that it still requires the business owner to run the business and often to generate the revenue.

Teenagers also have a habit of taking too many risks. Some pay off, but some don't, and these risks can be the making or breaking of your business. Because the business owner is still at the helm, there is also the risk that the lack of adequate management leads to the downfall of the business.

The next stage is the young adult. Those who don't take too many risks in the teenage years progress to making healthy sales and with stronger cash flow. That said, in the young adult stage, you'll find the processes and systems that tend to hold it back. To progress, business owners need to make the systems more scalable and repeatable. It is also the stage where the business owner is starting to step back from some of their roles, delegating more. It is at this stage that the profits start to appear.

If you make it through the young adult stage, you reach the mature adult stage. The prime of your life. At this stage, you have the systems in place to run the business smoothly. Strong growth can continue, but in a more sustainable fashion. The main characteristic here is that the business owner now has a management team in place, so that they are free to spend as little or as much time in the business as they choose.

It is at the mature adult stage that the business is worth the most. It is the most saleable, and this is essentially what we have been trying to move you towards through this book. Delegate to others, create amazing and repeatable systems and have handsome profits to show for it. The company becomes much less dependent on the founder.

This, sadly, is not the end. From here, the company can continue to age and reaches mid-life evaluation. Things begin to break down; the company loses its way a little as it continues to age. Old systems make it less and less dynamic.

From here, the business becomes an ageing business. Breakdown continues to accelerate. The problems in the business seem to be from external causes, not internal, and you blame others for the shortcomings. Your most talented people start to leave.

The next stage is institutionalization, where the organization is only kept alive through outside help like subsidization. Sadly, the stage after this is death.

Once the business progresses past mature adult, the stage at which the business is at its most valuable and in its prime, it is possible to return there. But the only way to do that is to innovate.

Let's take Apple as an example. After Steve Jobs was booted out of Apple in 1985, the company started to age. It came close to collapse, so was probably as far gone as institutionalization. Steve Jobs returned to Apple in 1997 and, in order to save it, he simplified the range, eliminating many of the options that customers had because they caused complexity. He then ramped up the innovation of the company, leading to the introduction of the iMac, then the iPod, iTunes, iPhone and then the iPad. It was through innovation that Steve brought Apple back from institutionalization, back to its prime.

Ironically, in the absence of Jobs, it could be argued that it has crept back into mid-life evaluation again, and maybe even an ageing company, as innovation has slowed. The introduction of the Apple Watch was less successful than expected and, at the point of writing, Apple shares are falling as a result of a decrease in iPhone sales. It has been knocked off the top spot of being the most valuable company in the world by Amazon, which, by the way, is constantly innovating with the introduction of gadgets like Alexa. If Apple wants to return to its former glory, it needs to innovate.

If you want to ensure that your company continues to grow and improve, you must ensure that you are constantly innovating. To use the words of Tony Robbins, "You need to strive for constant and never-ending improvement."

MARGINAL GAINS

David Brailsford, who headed up the British cycling team as it prepared for the London 2012 Olympics, where they won an amazing seven out of ten gold medals, talked about marginal gains. These marginal gains included customized aerodynamic helmets, hot pants worn between races to keep thigh muscles warm, sweat-resistant clothing, alcohol sprayed on the wheels at the start of the race to improve traction, and hypo-allergenic pillows. Not only did they select the right pillows, they selected the right beds and, after each day, they rolled them up and took them onto the next hotel to ensure that every night the cyclists and their support teams got the best night's sleep possible. Every little gain they could find got them a step closer to their goals through the compound effect.

The idea is that if you take each stage of the process you designed in the Phenomenal Process producer, an exercise in *The Entrepreneurial Happiness Workbook*, and improve it by 1%, you don't get a 1% gain. If it is a ten-step process, you get a 10% gain. As you might remember, our process has six steps. It's actually many more when you look at what goes on behind the scenes, but as far as the client is concerned, there are six stages. If we can increase each stage's efficiency by 5%, it will generate a 62% increase in our business.

INNOVATE, INNOVATE AND INNOVATE SOME MORE

How do you ensure that you constantly innovate? As with anything, there needs to be a strategy around it, and that is why we created our ENERGI meetings, which stands for 'energized never-ending revolutionary growth initiative.'

Once a month, relevant members of the team meet to work on improving the business. Some sessions are longer and some shorter, but 90 minutes would be a typical session.

We have a series of meetings that we work on over the course of the year, and more get added as we see processes and areas we need to work on. These meetings are about 'working on' the business, not 'working in' it. They are about bringing the team together to all identify ways in which we can continue to improve as a business. Some involve working on the behind-the-scenes things, some the client-facing work, some on the marketing and others on our values. Each one has a specific purpose and is a great way for us to improve what we do as a team.

As part of our Better Future coaching, we give you our ENERGI document, which contains the breakdown and all of the questions we work through in each of these ENERGI meetings. You can find out more about this at www.charliereading.com/BF.

WORKING ON THE BUSINESS

In additional to doing it as a team, it is essential for the business owner to put aside time each quarter to 'work *on* the business' as opposed to 'working *in* the business.' While I appreciate this is not the norm, it is the key to success for most successful businesses. After all, if you don't do it, you don't know if you are heading in the right direction.

When I first decided to get into triathlon, I had a lot to learn. I had spent the prior three years cycling more and more, setting myself long and longer challenges. When I first bought a bike as an adult, I signed up for a 100-mile charity bike ride from Rutland to the Norfolk coast, in order to give me the motivation to use it. I ended up completing that charity ride, but I was the only rider out of around 500 who did it on a mountain bike. I was on a steep learning curve that was steeper than the Rutland Hills. The following year I entered the London Surrey 100 mile and successfully completed that. The year after that I entered

The Dragon Ride, the 142-mile ride through both the Black Mountains and the Brecon Beacons in Wales. There were some serious climbs that day, and it was a tough challenge, but one I mastered all the same.

At the end of that year, when I was setting my goals for the year ahead, I needed something else, a new challenge. Should I find another ride that was longer and steeper or find something different? I decided I wanted to give triathlons a try and so, as I usually do, I set myself the three-year goal of completing an Ironman, something that seemed completely impossible given that I hadn't run or swam since school and was rubbish at both then. Based on this goal, though, I set a one-year goal of completing two sprint triathlons, one Olympic distance triathlon, and if those went OK, a half-Ironman in the year ahead.

Having got through the two sprints and one Olympic triathlon unscathed, The Vitruvian, my first half-Ironman coming at 1,900m swim, 85km bike and a 21km run, finally arrived. This was my big challenge for that first year, and I was determined to complete it. I thought the swim went fairly well and was enthusiastic getting onto the bike. As I left transition I got into the flow, and then turned on my bike computer. While looking down at the computer, not the road, I hit a speed bump and was sent flying. Blood dripping from my leg and elbow, I shook myself down, decided nothing on me or the bike was broken and headed on. Omitting that slight incident, the race went according to plan, and I finished in bang on six hours. Not fast, but I had finished.

When I set my goals for the following year, I concluded that my goal was to do the same events but to take off 5% off my times. Should I just train harder? It would have been very easy to say that I just needed to run more and further, cycle longer and swim more. That would work to a certain extent, but would it be enough and, if not, what was my alternative? Should I train smarter rather than harder? Work on my technique not just my fitness? I decided that time was already fairly stretched between work and family, and while I would train harder, I would definitely need to train smarter.

I started to analyse my workouts. My swimming worried me, as it had taken me 31 minutes to swim 1.5km and then 48 minutes to swim the 1.9km, so I started looking more closely at it. I realized that after a more detailed analysis, I hadn't actually swum 1.5km and 1.9km, I had swum over 10% more in both instances. On a swim that was supposed to be 1.5km, I had actually swum 1.8km. No wonder I was slow; I was swimming way farther than I needed to. The swim to the buoy, when looking at the map, veered all over the place and that added unnecessary distance to my swim.

On the bike, I looked at my bike set-up compared to others. I had a bike built for comfort on long rides, but everyone else had time-trial bars on their bikes, making them far more aerodynamic, plus fancy helmets that made them look like Sir Chris Hoy in the velodrome. On the run, I knew I had suffered from cramps, so I needed to research my nutrition and fluids to eliminate that risk.

So, what did I do? I read books on swim techniques, particularly around swimming in a straighter line; after all, one of the easiest ways to increase your swim speed is to cut the distance you swim. I changed my swimming stroke so that I breathed on both sides as opposed to the same side, and I practised sighting, the concept of looking up during your stroke to see your target. With regard to the bike, I invested in the right equipment to allow me to cut through the air much more easily. Finally, on the run, I read about nutrition and ways to eliminate the cramp risk.

When it came to The Vitruvian, one year later, I felt hopeful that I could get my time down from 6 hours to 5.43, which was the 5% reduction in my annual goals. What I did amazed even me.

On the day of the race, I told my family to get there expecting a five-hour and 30-minute finish, as I thought there was zero chance I would be any better than that. We have an ongoing joke about the fact that they missed me at the finish of pretty much all of my previous challenges, for one reason or another, so they didn't want to miss this one.

But they still did. I came sailing in after five hours and 15 minutes, a whopping 45 minutes quicker than the previous year, and way faster than I could have possibly hoped for. Not fast in some people's eyes, of course, but for me that was quick. Why did this happen though?

The reason I managed to knock 45 minutes off my previous years' time was because I chose to work on my approach, rather than just doing more training. My technique changes to my swimming reduced my swim distance, and that improved my speed, saving me a whopping 12% of my time. My changes to the bike and run each saved me around 5% on my previous time. Knowing what I know now, this could have been even more.

The point is that I was working on the business of training, as well as working in the business of training, and you need to do the same with your business. I was reading books, seeking the advice of other people with more experience than me and researching ways to improve the equipment I used. It would have been easier just to carry on running, cycling and swimming, in the hope that I got better, but it wouldn't have achieved the same results.

In business, it is so easy to get bogged down with clients' queries, emails and never-ending to-do lists, and that stops you improving the way you work. As a result, it is vital that you put time aside to work on the business. To look above the waterline and to see where you are going. After all, you may not be heading towards the buoy; you may be following another competitor out into open sea.

I make a point of always working at least one day a quarter on the business. In reality, as the business grows, one day a quarter isn't anywhere near enough. That could be on a specific course, but it can also be me locking myself in a room with a series of exercises to go through over the course of a day.

It used to be that I did this by myself, but I didn't get any of my team to take the same approach. After a helpful suggestion from a friend, I realized that we should be getting them to do this too. As a result, I now insist that everyone on the Efficient Portfolio team spends a minimum of one hour per month working on the business. This isn't their time at the ENERGI meeting, but this is time at their desk when they have to down tools, stop working and start thinking about how we can run our business better. That can be ways to improve the element of the business they work in, but it can also be ideas for areas of the business that they aren't even involved in.

It is limited to one page of A4, so that it doesn't take too long to go through the whole teams' ideas, but it has a number of benefits. First, they feel valued, as you are asking them for their opinion. Second, over the course of the month they are actively looking for ideas as to how we can improve the business, so that they have something to write about. It is a great way for new employees to give ideas that they see when they are new to the business, before they become indoctrinated into your processes. Finally, you can set themes, so one month it might be ways to create a better office environment or ways to become eco-friendlier.

I'd encourage you to build structure around how you and your team spend time working on the business to ensure you are getting to the finish line as quickly and efficiently as you possibly can.

LEARNING LIBRARY

Jim Rohn once said, "If you want a guaranteed strategy to become wealthy beyond your dreams, 25 years from now, all you need to do is read one book per week." I couldn't agree more.

By now, you should have worked out that I read a lot of books. If I want to improve an area of my life or my business, I find the best books to read, and then I action what I learn. I have found huge value in reading different books. Not only do I encourage my team to read these books, I promised to pay them more. I will never forget the day I came back from that holiday and told the team about that idea. I remember Charlotte, now my longest-standing employee, saying. "Did I hear you right? You are going to pay us more to read books? Count me in."

We created a structure that gave people a scale to ascend using titles like 'the wizard' and 'the guru,' and for every five books they read in the Learning Library, our little library of the books I had read that I thought would be valuable, we'd pay the team more.

Over the years, the team has read many of the top books that I have read and, as a result, they have grown more than I could have possibly hoped. They have learned so much quicker than I did because they were often given the tools earlier than I had found them.

This also sieves out the sponges from the rocks. In life, you meet some people that know it all and don't want to learn or improve themselves. These are your rocks. You also meet others who want to be the best they can be by learning as much as possible. These are your sponges. In my experience, you will have a much stronger, dynamic business if you have a team full of sponges. When you breed a culture of growth, a culture I'll talk more about in the next chapter, you need to find ways to identify the gems. Over time, hang onto the sponges, discard the rocks and your business will be far stronger for it. The Learning Library concept helps you find out who is a rock and who is a sponge.

The Learning Library also ties in really nicely with the concept of their working on the business. Once a team member has finished a book, the theme for their working on the business should be around what they have learned from that book that could be used to improve the business. I can't tell you how invigorating it is as a business owner to have your team regularly reading insightful business and personal development books and coming up with a flurry of new ideas. What better way to create a dynamic and motivated team than to have them learning and growing on the job?

I regularly get asked for book recommendations from people, inside our team and out, so you can find my top 12 business book recommendations at www.efficientportfolio.co.uk/books.

As long as you take action with what you read, it will transform your business. After all, 'growth' is one of our human needs, and if you are not growing you are dying. To put it another way, in the words of Ray Kroc, "When you are green you are growing, when you are ripe you rot."

UNILEVER'S NOZZLE

When it comes to innovating in your business, you can get caught up working out how best to do something. As I already mentioned, procrastination is a fear of starting, so it is often better to get on and try, but sometimes you need more than that.

In *Blackbox Thinking*, Matthew Syed looks at the story of Unilever. There are two morals to this story: first, the importance of innovation, but second, about not fearing mistakes through trial and error.

Unilever was facing a problem with its washing powder manufacturing process: a crucial nozzle required for this was continually failing. They employed the best engineers they could, but they were unabe to design a nozzle that worked any better. In an act of desperation, they decided to give the company's biologists a shot at fixing the problem. The biologists knew nothing about nozzles or the engineering that influenced it, but they did understand evolution, and they decided to apply that approach to this problem.

They took the failing nozzle and made 100 variations of it. They then took the best one from that experiment and made a further 100 variations of the chosen nozzle. They repeated this process until they eventually cracked it.

Why did they succeed despite the expert's failure? They succeeded because they failed fast!

You need to apply this approach to your marketing and to your business in general. You may not have any idea what the best solution or strategy is, but try as many different variations as you can, and as long as you measure the results and act based on those measurements, you can evolve a business process, solve a business problem or build an incredible marketing machine.

For example, with your marketing, rather than doing a single advert on Facebook, do three or even better, ten. Identify the one that converts the best and then create different variations of that. Do this again and again, and eventually you'll have an amazing marketing machine that you originally had no idea about.

But do not get caught up with trying to create perfection. Create something that works, get it out there and evolve from there. If you try and build the perfect business, you'll spend a lot of your time building stuff that turns out to be unimportant. Much better is to get a basic version of whatever you need out there, get people's feedback and work on the bits that they will appreciate.

For example, if you are setting up a new business, don't get too caught up with having fancy business cards, an all-singing and all-dancing website, the perfect logo or any gimmicks. Work out what the minimum viable product (MVP) is and only build that. For some businesses, that may simply be persuading someone to part with their cash for a service you are going to deliver.

The benefit of doing this is that you get to prove the concept first. You also can then get paid to build the rest of the concept, while making sure you build the bits that are most important to you. This approach even works for the big tech companies like Microsoft and Apple. When they release a new product, it is often fraught with problems and bugs. By essentially asking their audience to be their guinea pigs, you'd think they'd alienate their customers, but actually it turns them into raving fans.

For me, the best example of this is Tesla. I love my Tesla Model S. Not only is it a step towards ridding the world of fossil fuels and introducing the future of driverless cars, the vehicles are also constantly getting better and better. I often get into my car first thing in the morning to find out that there has been a software update, and my car just got better. This could be something serious, like improving the functionality of the autopilot feature, or it could be something less serious like the recent addition of emission testing mode, which essentially creates a whoopy cushion on one of the seats in the car, so that when you indicate, varying degrees of flatulence noises come out of the corner of the car's speaker.

While you could legitimately argue that adding farting sounds to the functionality hasn't improved the car or altered its value, the same could not be said about the improved autopilot. When I come to sell my car, I might be selling three-year-old hardware, of which there are only

35 moving parts, but I will also be selling brand-new software and features. The car is evolving with me and with the technology available, and I love it as a result. Like a fine wine, it is maturing with age.

As with most things, you can achieve most of what you need to do with 80% of the finished product. The remaining 20% takes so long to finish off and is often what gives you the 'headache' of finishing a project. I'd argue that you should forget the last 20% and get on and release at 80% or even less if possible. The feedback that you get from doing so will reshape what your 100% looks like anyway, and this way you will save time and wasted effort. In any project, work out what your MVP is and get on with rolling that out. Obviously do not put people at risk in doing so, but with the essentials covered, get it out there for the world to see. It may transform your end goal.

Learning, attending courses and reading is a way of evolving yourself. We don't quite know where we will end up as a result, but if we don't go through the process, one thing is for sure – that is, you won't evolve into anything better. In my Better Future coaching, I get people to do an exercise to help them work on what that should look like. You can find out more about this at www.charliereading.com/BF.

CHAPTER SUMMARY

- Improve what you do in your business by using regular ENERGI meetings with your team to work on the business.

- These can help you refine your customer facing processes, your back-office processes and turn you into a business of constant and never-ending improvement.

- See massive gains in what you achieve by finding ways to make small improvements in every step of your client journey through the 10 x 10 x 10 meeting.

- Avoid ageing as a business by looking at ways you can constantly innovate your way to success.

- Fail fast through 'blackbox thinking' so that through a process of elimination you can nail down the most successful strategy for the best results.

- Create a motivated and loyal team through constant and ongoing learning. Encourage your team to read new books by initiating a Learning Library in your business.

CHAPTER 14

GROW YOUR CULTURE

"Why did your product or company fail?" When posed with this question, people always give a permutation of the same three things: undercapitalized, the wrong people and bad market conditions. It's always the same three things. So, let's explore that.

With a purpose you will find a drive and, ultimately, reward and fulfilment, which leads to becoming a recipe for success, as in many cases throughout history. If you can harness just a small amount of that for yourself and your team, you will make a formidable opponent.

I often say to clients in the lead up to and at retirement, "If you want to create a happy retirement, you need enough money to be able to sleep at night, enough purpose to get you up in the morning and the health to allow you to do so." People in retirement often lose their purpose because it is very often linked to their job, so they need to put effort into creating a new purpose.

That said, many people in work have no purpose, which is why so many people are unhappy. According to Arnold Schwarzenegger, in his motivational speech that broke the internet, 74% of Americans hate their jobs. Apparently in the UK it is around 55%, if the CV Library study is to be believed. That means that most people spend most of their time doing something they hate. No wonder depression is on the rise.

Clearly defining your business purpose helps you all know why you are doing what you are doing. It comes back to what I talked about in Chapter 4, and it may well be the same as your 'why statement,' but you must keep reiterating this with your team. Not only that; ideally, they should help you create it so that they buy into it too. If your team truly believes in what you are doing as a business, and if they can see how you genuinely help people, they will buy into the company purpose and that will bring you a much stronger and more passionate team.

In addition to your team knowing why they do what they do, they should also know why you go about your business in the way you do. This will define what it means to be part of your team. This is called your company culture. It was vital we built it together as a team, rather than me tell everyone what the culture was. Within days of defining our company culture at Efficient Portfolio, I could sense a difference in the business. It was as if everyone was walking around the office with their shoulders pulled back just a little more than a few days earlier. They were standing taller, and they were acting with more pride. They had more purpose, and they were working better as a result.

What does it mean to be part of your business? Do you know? You might think you know, but is that what your employees think, because that might be very different. Will a new employee fit in with your current team and the ethos of the business? These are all questions that can be answered by building a company culture.

We review our company culture every year, as you saw when I talked about our ENERGI meetings. That is one of the ENERGI meeting topics, so once a year we spend time talking about it and refining it. That said, it hasn't really changed much since we first created it, which makes me feel it is pretty close to the mark. Here is our current company culture, which we call the EP Code (for Efficient Portfolio).

E	Embrace fun and be a little quirky
P	Pursue growth and learning
C	Constant and never-ending improvement
O	Open and honest relationships
D	Deliver WOW through client service
E	Energized, positive and passionate team

We have this on our walls, we have it in our team planner document that we review weekly together, and we have it in our 'culture book.' Once a year we produce a hardback photo book of what it means to be part of Efficient Portfolio. There are quotes from the team, an explanation of each point of the EP Code and our values. This book is a wonderful record of what the business looked like years ago, but it is also a fantastic thing to have in your company reception for people to look at. What better way to tell your new prospects about your business and the culture within it?

Having now witnessed its impact for a number of years, I believe that having a company culture has a similar effect. Essentially, you are programming into the minds of your team how they need to act to be part of the team. As long as that is good for them, as well as you, that has got to be a fantastic thing.

Finally, in case you didn't now have enough reasons to document a company culture, here's one more. If you want to recruit as well as Google does, you need to know your company culture. Google bases their interview process around their company culture and so, in recent years, we have done the same. We tell candidates what our culture is and ask them to give examples of how they have exhibited these qualities in the workplace.

This does two things. First, those who genuinely fit your culture will be excited. This will not only be evident in the interview process but means that they will go home and decide that they really want to work for you. After all, you have to sell this job to them as well as they sell themselves to you. Second, from their answers you'll get a feel for whether they are likely to actually fit your culture. In my experience, it is the people who don't fit the company culture who end up causing you the most grief, even if they are brilliant at their roles. It is good to spot this early on and save everyone a lot of pain and disruption. Once you have a company culture documented, build your recruitment process around it.

It also makes sense to look at this retrospectively. Look at your current team and assess them against each of your culture traits. You may be surprised by what you see. It may well be that this process highlights something that in your gut you already knew. The one or two team members who just don't seem to fit in will become obvious. For everyone's benefit, you'll probably find that they are better served by working elsewhere.

I encourage you to set aside at least a couple of hours to put together your company culture. As a team, brainstorm what you think it means to be part of your company; pick the best ones and create something amazing from them. With company culture, you can grow something incredible.

CODE OF HONOUR

For your team to succeed, it's important to have a code of honour, having a rulebook that the team plays by. The company culture is about how we conduct ourselves as a business. A code of honour is more about how we act towards our fellow team members. A number of years ago, we put together our code of honour, and again through our ENERGI meetings over the years we have refined it to the following:

We praise more than we criticize.
We never leave a team member behind.
We are always punctual, professional and prudent.
We look forwards, not back.
We treat others how we want to be treated.
We don't make excuses; we find solutions.

On a number of occasions, as inevitably happens when employing a team, people have overstepped the mark or have been letting their team members down. The code of honour allows you to easy highlight why there is a problem. You can even make their code of honour performance part of their bonus structure if you so wish, as we have done a couple of times. It's essentially a way of saying, "Are you playing as part of the team?" If they aren't, it allows that team member to consider why they are not hitting the mark.

As a business owner, a code of honour isn't something you should just create and inflict on your team. You need to work on it as a team, as it will have far more power and meaning, and everyone will take ownership of it. So, create a code of honour and then incentivize people to stick to it.

THE MOONSHOT

I first heard the term 'Moonshot' from Peter Diamandis, but I believe it actually originates as a term used by Astro Teller, who is the CEO of X (formerly Google X). Most entrepreneurs out there are trying to grow their business by 10%. Astro is focused on looking at growing the business by ten times, which is quite a massive difference.

If you want to grow your business by ten times, you need to think differently. You need a completely different mindset, and that is achieved by creating a Moonshot.

In May 1961, President John F. Kennedy announced the almost insane goal of putting a man on the moon by the end of the decade. The technology wasn't even close to being ready to achieve this. Nobody knew how it could happen, and yet this first Moonshot was achieved just eight years later. It was a huge goal but, as a result, people had to think very differently.

Steve Jobs' greatest trait was probably that he could see things that his customers didn't even know they wanted or needed. "A thousand songs in your pocket" was a pipedream so far from what we had been used to, we didn't know we needed or wanted it, and yet now it is an essential part of life for most people. The smartphone even more so. The iPad, unbelievably successful, was just another example of 10x thinking, as when Jobs came up with the concept the technology just wasn't there to make it possible. But with that in mind, he forced it through as soon as it was feasible.

If you want to grow your business, you need a Moonshot. If you want a culture in your business where everyone is pulling towards that growth, again you need a Moonshot.

At Efficient Portfolio, our Moonshot is to help one million people through financial planning. At the moment, if you took every financial planner in the UK combined, they could not cope with delivering financial planning to one million people. I genuinely have no idea how I can make this happen yet; however, I do know it will be possible. I haven't been presented with the right opportunity to make this happen, but I have no doubt it will come at some point. The universe has a habit of showing you the way, you just have to tell it what you want. A Moonshot is a simple way of communicating this mind-blowing goal to your team, to your subconscious and to the outside world. Who knows, writing it down here may be the next step in us achieving our Moonshot.

Again, decide on this with your team. Clearly, as the entrepreneur, you will have a strong sway on this one, but they do need to buy into it, otherwise you will be trying to do a moon landing all by yourself.

CHAPTER SUMMARY

- Build a better business by determining what it means to be a part of your business.

- By understanding what the culture of your business is, you can work better together, recruit better people and understand more clearly when someone doesn't fit into your team.

- Have a stronger team by creating a code of honour for your team, so that they all treat each other with the respect that you all would expect.

- Have your whole team driving towards a bigger better future by having a clearly defined Moonshot.

CHAPTER 15

PRIOR PLANNING PREVENTS

Caryl and I are big fans of eating out. Over the years, we have been fortunate enough to have eaten at some amazing national and international Michelin-starred restaurants. Many of these restaurants have been brilliant; but some have been distinctly underwhelming. Over time, if I am honest, the novelty has worn off because we find that too many are of a similar ilk and just don't stand out.

Don't get me wrong; the food is lovely, and at the time you enjoy the occasion, but very few are truly memorable life experiences. However, one that does not fall into that category was 'The Fat Duck,' Heston Blumenthal's restaurant in Bray. For as long as I live, I will not forget that evening.

Set in the heart of the Berkshire countryside, this village is unbelievably home to not one, but three Michelin-starred restaurants: The Fat Duck and The Hind's Head, both owned by Heston Blumenthal and Michel Roux's Waterside Inn.

What made this such a special experience is prior planning by them and us. This was a special place to eat and very difficult to get a table, so we had waited until Caryl's 40th to treat ourselves and two sets of friends, the Olivers and the Wadas. The prior planning by us involved making sure that three months to the day before we wanted to dine, we were online securing a table the second they went live. If you don't, you miss out. We booked ourselves into a hotel that was just a short taxi ride away. We planned the evening: meet at the hotel bar for some champagne, followed by cocktails in another of Heston's establishments, 'The Crown,' then on to The Fat Duck for a memorable evening, and all topped off by Sunday lunch in The Hind's Head the following day.

The prior preparation by the team at The Fat Duck was much more detailed. Already awarded 'The best restaurant in the world award' in 2008, 2009 and 2010, they didn't want to rest on their laurels, so in 2015 they closed for six months while they completely redesigned most of their menu. How many restaurants take their menu that seriously? Very few.

We were lucky enough to be joining them in May 2016, not long into their new menu. According to the critics, their prior planning had paid off, as the food and experience was apparently even better than before. When we booked the table, we had to pay for everyone's food upfront. The only time I have had to do that! More prior planning.

As the organizer, soon after booking I received an email from the restaurant. Nothing unusual there, I thought, until I opened it. I was being sent on a journey and was asked to answer a number of questions about each of the guests: which football team they supported, their business interests, etc. All of this sounded irrelevant to me at this stage, but soon all would become clear.

Now, I would not want to give away the magic of the experience, in case you ever decide to visit yourself. It would be such a shame to spoil the surprise, so all I can really say is that we were blown away. By the 5th of 17 courses, we'd already run out of superlatives. At different stages of the meal we had guests in tears – tears of joy as they were overwhelmed by the food and the experience.

Planning that meal to the finest of details: taking us on a journey creates the most wonderful of experiences. While the food is amazing, it is only part of it. It is the show, the theatre and, ultimately, the preparation that allows the team at The Fat Duck to deliver a night none of us will ever forget. It is all in the planning, and the same applies to your business.

THE LEADERSHIP TEAM

In Chapter 12, I talked about the limitless life planner. This is about planning a better future by making commitments to yourself of the things you will achieve. The amazing thing about the limitless life planner is that when you break your life up into three-month periods, you can achieve so much more. Three months just seems to be the right frequency. Any more frequent, and you give it less attention; do it less thoroughly, and you create fewer inspiring commitments and fall off the wagon.

I write out my own goals every quarter, and even when I had a break from attending the workshops, I continued to do this. I revamped how I structured my goals with the help of work from people like Brian Tracy and Tony Robbins, and I created a structure that worked really well for me. Originally, these were all bunched together, but with the help of Tony Robbins, as you've now seen, they were broken up into personal goals and business goals, and even separated out into the different roles I play in my life.

But there was me setting my own personal goals every quarter, and also helping the team set theirs, but were we setting business goals as a team? No, we weren't. So I created the leadership team. By appointing my leadership team, I have given some of my key team members the responsibility and authority to lead elements of my business, and the results have paid dividends.

Since creating the leadership team, I have seen a massive step up in how these guys and girls act inside the business. How they deal with problems, and how they move the business forwards, because they understand and are bought into the company's goals much more than ever before. So how do we achieve that?

Our leadership team meet every quarter, for a full day. Ideally, this needs to be outside of your office. At the bare minimum, you need to be locked away in a meeting room undisturbed for the whole day, also stepping out for lunch, so there is no temptation to check your emails. The agenda, which is derived from Gino Wickman's *Traction*, can be downloaded from here www.charliereading.com/leader.

You will see that I mention here 'the one-page business plan' a few times. This is our adaption of so many other things, and where we bring a lot of what we do together. You can download a copy of it on the same page too.

The one-page business plan covers our core values, The EP Code, our why statement and our Moonshot. This means that each quarter, as a minimum, the leadership team revisits and rereads what these are. That doesn't mean we tweak them each quarter, far from it, but it is acting as a reminder as to what we are trying to achieve, and how we are going to get there. The document also covers a summary of our marketing strategy for the year, our ten-year targets and what makes us unique. Finally, and most importantly for the purpose of the leadership meetings, it covers our goals: three-year, one-year and quarterly, plus our issues that need solving for that quarter.

The first part of the leadership meeting is spent reviewing what's working and what's not, how we got on achieving last quarter's goals and what issues have cropped up in the business. The second part of the meeting is then about identifying the goals for the next quarter, some of which will have rolled over from the previous quarter. The next part of the day is about going through the issues in order of importance and working out solutions and strategies for each. For each solution, we add this to the goals for the quarter.

Finally, we assign each element of the goals between the leadership team members. That doesn't mean they have to do them themselves, but it does mean they are responsible for making sure they are done.

By taking this approach, I have a far more organized team, a better business and more free time too! My leadership team knows what page we are on, and they are pulling in the same direction as me. By having clearly defined goals for the business, over the next quarter, year and three years, they know the bigger picture, so they can make the right judgements with that in mind.

You may wonder, as I did, whether there would be enough to talk about for a whole day. We have never failed to fill the time. In *Traction*, Gino Wickman suggests that you also have an annual meeting (ideally at the end of the year) that is conducted over two days. For this meeting, the agenda continually evolves and again the latest version can be found at www.charliereading.com/leader.

Essentially, this is the same as the quarterly meeting with a few extra additions. As it is the annual meeting, in addition to reviewing your quarterly goals, you need to revisit and revamp and visualize your three-year goals and you need to create new one-year goals. You also need to conduct a SWOT analysis, and I like to do a summary of a book I have read, too.

I encourage you to create your leadership team. What that looks like will depend on your own business. Build the one-page business plan with them, and then meet each quarter so that it evolves with your ever-changing business. At the start you may need to put aside longer to get that done, especially if you have not done any of this before, but I promise that you will not be disappointed with the results.

THE BRAIN TRUST

Being a fan of Steve Jobs, I was keen to read Ed Catmull's *Creativity, Inc.*, as Steve had such a huge impact at Pixar. He ploughed pretty much everything he had made from Apple into this studio. At times it seemed like this would backfire, but eventually it proved to be one of the best decisions he made.

One thing that struck me about Pixar (and some of it was definitely Jobs' influence) was that it was a forward-thinking company. Part of this was that each week they had a meeting called 'the brain trust.' Named after the key people that Franklin Roosevelt surrounded himself with during his presidential administration, this was a meeting each Monday where Pixar thrashed out the week's issues.

At the time, at Efficient Portfolio we were already meeting every Monday morning to talk about any issues in the business and also to make sure we all knew what the most important things each of us was doing that week. Calling it the brain trust didn't change anything other than the story behind it, thus the feel. The whole Efficient Portfolio team now meets for the brain trust every Monday morning. It's always at the same time, which means we even have a voicemail set up that automatically tells people that's why we aren't answering at that time.

In this meeting, we always cover the following agenda, which can again be found at www.charliereading.com/leader.

Again, we start off with the best things that have happened in the week. Always start meetings on a positive – it gets everyone into the right mindset and allows you to celebrate your successes.

Next, we talk about the successful business scorecard, plus the business' quarterly goals, so we can remind ourselves exactly what we are trying to hit and what we are all working towards. A communicated goal is 100% more likely to be followed through.

We then look at what is happening in the business for the week ahead, so we are all aware of any events or companywide meetings that are happening. Nothing worse than one of your team wandering in looking less smart than usual as 15 new prospective clients sit in reception waiting for a seminar.

That's followed by going through a team planner, which is a crucial but simple tool we use to track people's accountability. Finally, we each list the three most important results we need to achieve that week. This is so that everyone knows what we need to do that week, so we all know where we stand and can collaborate on any overlapping projects.

It is a simple meeting, which usually lasts no more than 30 minutes, and keeps us all in tune with what is happening in the company. As we've grown as a business, it has helped us all remain close as a team. These weekly meetings working *in* the business are then complemented by the monthly ENERGI meetings where we are working *on* the business.

I recommend you schedule in your own version of the brain trust meeting once a week. We like Mondays, as it gets the team on track for the week ahead. Diarize your brain trust and help bring out the monsters in your Inc.!

CHAPTER SUMMARY

- Have a more saleable, better-run and more dynamic business by creating a leadership team in your business.

- Nurture these leaders so that they can drive your business forwards through quarterly structured leadership meetings.

- Generate more efficient teamwork work through establishing the most important things that need to happen that week through the weekly brain trust meeting.

CHAPTER 16

THE END GAME

In the week leading up to the birth of Ffion, our first child, we found out that she was pointing in the wrong direction. She was what is known as a breech baby, which can lead to many more problems and risks at birth, both for baby and mum. As a result, Caryl ended up having an emergency C-section. Not something we had planned for, and a more clinical and worrying entrance into the world for our first born. The main thing, of course, is that both Caryl and Ffion emerged from it safely.

What that meant, though, was that when it came to the birth of our second child, much of the childbirth experience was still new to us. We went through the stages at home with the tens machine providing little to no pain relief. We had the drive into hospital, worrying that we were going too soon, but also worrying that we had left it too late.

The birth didn't go according to plan, and while I will spare you the details, it was more drawn out than it should have been. To steal a popular phrase among the partners of those giving birth, "It was like watching your favourite pub burn down!" After a long, drawn-out birth, I started to feel a little queasy.

I've never been great with blood and gore, which is ridiculous as a farmer's son. I can still vividly remember the humiliation of going green in an A-level biology lesson where we had had to prick our finger with a pin to extract a drop of blood to analyse under the microscope. What made matters worse was the fact that we had to head through to a second classroom to view the results on a TV screen. There was me, in front of not just one classroom of children but two, told to sat on the floor for fear of me collapsing. All over a single droplet of my own blood.

Anyway, back to the birth of our second child. As a result of feeling queasy, I took a seat next to Caryl, so when our second born finally arrived, I saw baby's entrance into the world through the arch of Caryl's legs. I have to admit that the next few minutes remain a little blurry as to the exact proceedings, but I definitely remember passing up the opportunity to cut the umbilical cord; that would have been the straw that broke the camel's back. Then I remember the midwife asking me to tell Caryl whether we had a boy or a girl. Of this I was certain; I had seen the evidence.

"We have a boy, a beautiful baby boy," I proclaimed. Having come armed with names to suit both sexes, we announced him to the world as Euan, and he was wrapped up and passed to Caryl for her first cuddle. How perfect, a little baby brother to Ffion. The next steps were obvious. I called my parents and told them of the exciting news. Brenda, Caryl's Mum was with us at the time, so I phoned Russell, her father, to again share the wonderful news.

After about 20 minutes, the midwife came back into the room and asked if she could weigh baby Euan.

"What a lovely name," she remarked, as she wrapped him up to put him onto the scales.

At which point she let out a small scream. What had happened? What was wrong? As a new parent, it is moments like this that seem to last a lifetime. Was there a problem with his breathing? Had she somehow hurt him, or could something else, even more worrying, be wrong? These thoughts flashed through your mind at 100 mph.

"I am afraid," she said, "that you do not have a baby boy at all. You do, in fact, have a beautiful baby girl."

What? How? But I saw ... clearly after ten years the memories have faded a little, but I remember being 100% sure of what I had seen. Obviously, I knew that there would be an umbilical cord, after all, I had done A-level biology! I know what I saw, and it was the evidence required to sign off our new baby as a boy. And yet, what I saw didn't actually exist. It was never there.

Fortunately, Bronwyn, as she was named after a fleeting 20-minute spell as Euan, was born early in the morning. As a result, I got straight back on the phone to my mum and father-in-law to correct my small but life-defining error. Thank goodness Bronwyn was born early in the morning, as otherwise it would have probably taken about three hours to get through to Mum on the phone, by which time most of the East Midlands would have known we had been blessed with a baby boy, and she may have already submitted the congratulatory notice to the local paper.

The important point is that our eyes do deceive us. I was sure of what I saw, and yet it wasn't ever there. It was my brain, eyes or something playing tricks on me. It is very easy for this to happen in your business. We think something is going well, as from the outside it appears that way. It is only through closer inspection that we can identify where our initial instincts and judgements are floored.

I hope that this book helps you see some of the areas you can improve in the way that you approach your business, but there is one final piece of the jigsaw needed to clearly know where you are heading: what is the End Game?

We have started to think about this more with the goals that we created as part of the limitless life planner. If you haven't done this already, it is so important you complete this now. This gives you some clear areas to aim towards. Try and make these as SMART as you can, i.e., specific, measurable, attainable, relevant and timely. These should continue to evolve with you, though. The more you think about them, the more you can refine them. It is sometimes difficult to clearly think about what you want to be, because it is so difficult to think about life ten years from now.

In my first few days at Newcastle University, I was introduced to Rob, and another 'Agric' (Agriculture student). Like me, Rob was not a typical farmer's son, and not a typical Agric.

He didn't wear cords and check shirts but instead, growing up in Cornwall, had more of a lean towards baggy surfer trousers and skater shoes. Instead of wanting to drink beer through a sheep's oesophagus, as the Agrics were renowned for, he'd rather head off to a DJ set to dance the night away. While that wasn't me initially, spending more time hanging out with him, it soon became me. As much as he rubbed off on me, I did him. He hated football when he arrived in Newcastle; but a combination of my enthusiasm for it, Euro '96 'coming to the Toon' and the infectious Geordie devotion to their team, The Magpies, soon had him turning into a massive England and Newcastle fan.

Rob was an incredible guy. As quick as he was to take the mickey out of his friends, he was also always on hand to help them, and to have a laugh in the process. While he wasn't a typical farmer, unlike me he had a massive passion for farming. He loved his dairy herd and would spend nearly as much time at uni finding cattle to buy for the herd at home as he would leading me astray. He loved his cows so much that, when I had my 21st birthday party back at our farm in Rutland, instead of showing up with a girlfriend, he arrived with a cow in a trailer that needed a stable for the night.

After university, he headed back to the farm in Cornwall, where he started to expand the herd. After uni, while I was travelling, he decided he wanted to join me for a while. We had an amazing couple of months travelling through Thailand and Malaysia, doing full moon parties, learning to dive and trekking through Chiang Mai together, something that inspired him to go on to travel more too.

I was his best man when he married Sam, a girl at uni who I had introduced him to. Sadly, that marriage didn't last, but he maintained his love for farming. He started to expand the farm into projects like yoghurt drinks, a veal unit with his sister and anaerobic digestion unit with his brother.

I have no doubt that the former of these would now be a household name had what happened next not come to pass.

While his failed marriage to Sam had hit him hard, he got back on track, and Rob was settling down with a new girlfriend and her daughter. Sarah shared his passion for the farm, and Rob was starting to blossom again. On a research trip to Scandinavia with his dad and brother, his divorce from Sam finally came through, and he confessed to his brother that upon his return he would propose to Sarah. Life was starting to take shape again for this incredible guy.

The very next day, Rob and a pilot took a plane for a tour of the anaerobic digestion plant they had travelled to see for research. As his brother and dad watched on, the plane nosedived into the ground on landing. Rob and the pilot were killed instantly.

The news reached me through one of Rob's Cornish friends I had met when organizing his stag do. Obviously, we were all shocked beyond belief. He was 30 years old. He had made such a huge impression on so many people during that relatively short time, we were bound to be. I was honoured to be asked to say a eulogy at his funeral. Probably the toughest public speaking I'll ever do. As we walked out of the church that day, with the sound of Fat Les' football anthem 'Vindaloo' playing in the aisles, I had a thought: *This could just as easily be my funeral. I have been on such a similar journey to Rob, why was it him and not me, or someone else?* Then I thought, *what would this day look like had it been me? What would people think of the 30 years I have spent on this planet? What have I achieved at this point? Would they be proud?* Suddenly, it made me think about my life differently. None of us know how long we will be on this Earth, so we have got to get on and live the life we want. This isn't a practice run, we've got to grab life by the proverbials and get on and live the best life we can. There are no second chances.

Take a few minutes to visualize your last hours on Earth and your funeral. See the people you care most about sitting by your bedside for your last moments. Those same people and more attending your burial and at the wake afterwards. By looking at the end of your life, I hope it highlights the blessings that surround you today. It should also help you evaluate your life thus far and consider whether you have done the things you want to be remembered for. After imagining the end of your life, you're less likely to think, "I should have spent a few more hours in the office or replied to my emails a little more promptly."

Then, take a few minutes to think about what your company could look like ten years from now. Imagine your company is 10x bigger than it is today, or maybe 100x bigger. Think big. What would it look like?

These are a couple of exercises that maybe could help you to create the best life you can that I do in my Better Future coaching. You can find out more about this at www.charliereading.com/BF.

MITIGATE RISK

Part of planning for the End Game is also trying to mitigate risk. It is all very well having this great plan for the future, but one thing is for sure, unexpected things are going to happen along the way that are going to mess this up. It may be big things, and it may be little things, but technologies will disrupt markets, people will quit, fall ill or worse, and fashions will change. As a result, if you want to give yourself the best chance possible of achieving a result, you've got to look at how much risk is involved.

In looking at business opportunities, I look at whether there is a 3:1 risk. I believe that if there is not three times the upside to the downside, then it isn't worth doing. Ultimately, none of us know whether something will be a success or not, but if you keep trying things, some will come off and some will inevitably fail. If you have three times as much upside to downside, the ones that work, which hopefully will be most, will reward you sufficiently well to make you some money and to offset the ones that don't.

The same applies to when you are investing your money. You need to see that over the long term the investment returns are likely to be sufficient to offset the risks. Too many people take too much risk with their money when it comes to investing. What they don't realize is that often they take unnecessary risks. Investing successfully, as I pointed out in Chapter 7, is about getting the best growth possible for a level of risk you understand and are comfortable with. It is about protecting yourself in the hard times and benefiting from the growth in the good times. Diversification, thus risk mitigation, allows you to keep your plans on track.

There are certain unknowns you can't plan for, though. You insure your office, your car and your laptop to make sure that if something happens to them, you are protected and not stuck with the bill. If you were to buy anything worth a significant amount of money, you'd want to know it was insured before you even got it home, so why don't we think of people in the same way? After all, it is people, certainly for now, who generate our income, our capital and run our business.

If you multiply your earnings by the number of years you plan to work, that is how much you are worth, in today's money. Again, ignoring inflation, someone who earns £22,000 at age 20 will have generated £1m of income by the time they retire at 65. That is ignoring inflation and pay rises. If you had an asset worth £1m, I'm guessing you'd want to insure it. The question is, who is at risk?

One Tuesday evening in May 2007, I was playing golf with my usual group. One of them, a keen dabbler in picking shares, collared me on the first tee.

"Have you heard that Philip Carter has died?" he said.

"Philip who?" I replied.

"The MD of Carter and Carter, the training company that's based in Peterborough." As soon as someone talks to me about their money in this way, I know a question is coming next. "So, Charlie, do you think I should sell my shares in Carter and Carter?"

At the time, I knew nothing of this company, or the man who ran it, so I offered my generic advice in this instance: "That depends on how well he has set the company up, and how he has mitigated risks like his own death."

Philip Carter was a non-executive director of Chelsea FC. Like his chairman, Matthew Harding, he sadly died in a helicopter crash coming back from a Chelsea match, although this was not the same crash. He left behind his wife and children. His day job was running Carter and Carter, a highly successful training company that was valued at £500 million the day before his death.

The shares dropped in value by about 20% on the news of his death, but within six months the shares had fallen from £12.75 to 85p and were suspended on the stock exchange. Less than 12 months later, in April 2008, the administrators were called in and the business folded.

His wife, instead of inheriting a business worth £500m, got nothing; the employees were out of a job; and had there been other shareholders in the business, they would have lost their stakes too.

This is just one example of a risk associated in people that business owners often overlook, but what could have been done to offset this risk? One thing is known as Key Person Insurance. When something unexpected happens, like the death or serious illness of a shareholder or key member of the team, people get worried. The bank gets worried and may call in the overdraft. Creditors get worried and may pull your credit. Customers get worried and may be tempted to switch to your competitors who you can guarantee will be swooping around like vultures. Employees get worried, as they have lost one of their key leaders. All this can put a business as successful as Carter and Carter out of business.

Key Person Insurance would have injected capital into the business to alleviate worries and provide liquidity in the short term, while replacements were recruited. This isn't just about the business owner either. What about your top salesperson? Will you lose their business? What about a key member of your leadership team? In addition to having protection in place to help support the business, having protection in place to support the business owner's family would have also made sense. Finally, what if there's a business partner? The business owner's partner would probably have wanted to sell the shares, and the business partner may want to buy them, so capital to allow that to happen too would also have helped.

Being a business owner is about taking risks; otherwise, you'd almost certainly be employed. That said, the best business owners only take calculated risks and, where possible, they mitigate those risks.

I was talking to a client about this earlier on this morning. He is a successful guy, with a young family who are privately educated. In order to cover his sizeable mortgage, to provide an income for him and the family in the event of illness, and to provide money for school fees in the event of his death, we were talking about some fairly high costs of around £1,000 per month. Initially, this sounds like a lot. He has ten years until his youngest is through school, so he really has a ten-year risk window, where if something happens to him, it would blow up the plan. Over those ten years, the protection is likely to cost him around £120,000. That said, if something happens to him, or worse to him and his wife, the risk to his children is around £3.5m. While £120,000 sounds like a lot, it doesn't when you look at the risk if something were to happen.

However, there are a lot of financial protection products that I would avoid like the plague. Things that are renowned for not paying out at the time that you need them. After all, the most expensive insurance you can have is the one that doesn't pay out when you need it. The best suggestion I can give you is to seek the advice of a truly independent financial planner, like the ones we have at Efficient Portfolio. That way you can benefit from the wisdom of our experience, as opposed to finding out the hard way when it's too late.

MERGE FUN WITH BUSINESS

Enough talk about death and illness; let's move onto something more fun. No one said work cannot be fun. In fact, we should be doing everything possible to make sure that work is as much fun as possible. As you've worked out, I love to swim, cycle and run. I also love to scuba-dive and play golf. In fact, anything that can include all of those activities would rank pretty highly on my list.

I recently was lucky enough to be able to attend a conference for the top financial planners from around the world that was held in Los Angeles. Given the time difference and the fact that I'd never been to LA before, I wanted a day either side of the event to acclimatize and take a look around. I'd heard loads about it, but never been before. I had a thought: *what better opportunity to see the area than to hire a bike and explore, while picking off some of my training for my next triathlon?* So, I did just that.

Finding a decent bike to rent was a challenge enough, but then trying to identify where to cycle was essentially a dice roll. I read up online, looked at Strava routes, asked friends who had been and contacted the local cycle shops for some recommendations. Eventually, I settled on Palos Verdes for an 80-mile circuit for before the event, and Malibu including Mulholland Drive for a 100-mile route afterwards. Both looked and sounded like stunning rides, but I was heading into a completely unknown world.

After collecting my bike, I headed out towards Palos Verdes, the most expensive real estate in LA. I got chatting to a local at some lights and ended up cycling with him for the first 20 or so miles. It turned out he was also a financial planner of sorts so, combined with his cycling trips to Europe, we had loads to chat about while we cycled the streets and coastline of LA. He gave me top tips of where to buy coffee and lunch in Palos Verdes, and my ride out was perfect. I took in stunning cliff-top views over the Atlantic while cycling past incredible but surprisingly understated houses – not at all what I expected from LA. I saw volleyball on Redondo, muscles on Venice Beach and even dolphins on Manhattan Beach. It was a brilliant day's cycling, combined with a delicious seafood lunch overlooking the Atlantic Ocean.

However, the day cycling in Malibu wasn't quite as successful. I realized over the course of my stay in LA that cycling from Santa Monica along the Pacific Coast Highway was going to be risky business. For the first 20+ miles of my route, I feared for my life as I dodged gas-guzzling juggernauts, so decided to swap my bike for a ride in a friendly Uber taxi. Once in Malibu, I jumped back on the bike and headed up into the hills and canyons. It was hot, unsurprisingly, and what remained of my route was nothing but climbing and descending. The views were stunning, the cycling some of the best I've done, and the conditions perfect, but again things didn't go according to plan.

I discovered that my planned pit stop only opened on the weekend, so I had no chance to refuel or fill the water bottle.

My next option of a stop amazingly didn't have a shop, garage or even an ice cream van anywhere to be seen. Twice over the course of my route I had to wander into a random vineyard and, while they didn't have food to buy that was of any use to me, they kindly allowed me to refill my water bottles. After all, with all this climbing and hot sun, I was getting through a lot of it. Instead of my wonderful 100-mile day of cycling through the mansions of Malibu, I ended up somewhat stressed and hungry.

And that's just the cycling. I ran some interesting routes around LA on the mornings of my conference; never really knowing whether the gangland LA I heard about in rap music was around the next corner. I didn't brave a sea swim, as I just couldn't find the research to tell me it was safe, and the hotel pool proved to only be open while I was at the conference.

So, why was my first day of cycling so much better than my second? I think it was partly down to the fact that I met that local. The conversation, his local knowledge, and the companionship was the difference between my successful Palos Verdes cycling versus my unsuccessful Malibu adventure, and that got me thinking: wouldn't it have been amazing if I could have easily found a group of local cyclists who were around the same pace as me and who were heading out around the time I was? I know that if the shoe was on the other foot, I would love to act as tour guide for the day to a traveller staying in my part of the world. Joining up with a local group of keen pedallers could have made my LA cycling even more special and avoided me making my Malibu mistakes.

In addition to my cycling, perhaps I could have also run with a local running group, who'd have taken me on the best and safest routes the city had to offer. Perhaps an open water swimming group could have given me the confidence to explore the LA waters too.

But every cloud has a silver lining. This trip inspired me to create a new business called www.Tribeathlon.com. It connects you to other's training sessions, so that whether you are looking for training buddies at home, or locals while you're on holiday, you can find companions of a similar ability and the same goals.

Over the years I have found fellow cyclists, runners and swimmers to be some of the friendliest people I know. It seems to go with the territory. Miles are our meditation, and that seems to make them nice people. Tribeathlon. com allows you to find the 'tribes' that already exist, wherever in the world you are, so you can enjoy your training to the max.

Tribeathlon.com has been a way of me making more of my work life about the things I love. In time I plan for it to mean I spend more time in that world. I am trying to merge my fun with my business life, because no one said work can't be fun.

In addition to this, by going to the global conference in LA, I not only got to learn how I can improve my business, but I got to cycle and run my way around an incredible part of the world for the first time. This year's conference, just a few weeks away, is being held in Miami. Not only am I attending it, I am now speaking at it, sharing some of these ideas with 12,500 of the top financial advisers from around the world. Of course, I have planned my Free Days® there too: two days of cycling along the Miami coastline and one day of diving with lemon, tiger and hammerhead sharks. Now that for me is merging business with fun.

This may sound like a holiday, but for me it isn't. While cycling for roughly 16 hours, I will be listening to business books and coming up with ways to improve our business over the next year. While travelling to and from the diving, while flying, and while running along Miami Beach

I'll be doing exactly the same. I see this time as an amazing opportunity to brainstorm ideas of how I can take Efficient Portfolio to the next level. Not just from the top speakers and spending time with my peers, but through a total immersion in learning while I am away. In fact, this is actually what Bill Gates and Steve Jobs, to name but a few, were doing at the peak of their careers. Taking a week out of their business to travel to somewhere that allowed them to read, think and set up the next set of goals for their business. It didn't serve them too badly, now, did it?

What I have realized over time is that my primary role in our businesses is to think and come up with ideas for others to implement. The wonderful thing about that is that thinking can be done anywhere. It can be done in different parts of the world, while doing different activities, and can be stimulated in different ways. That means there is more opportunity to merge fun with work.

Finally, I know that the golf club is a great place to meet new clients. I don't actively go looking for them, but over the course of a four-hour round of golf, you cannot help but talk about what you do, and that leads to opportunities. So, leaving early one day a week to play golf not only makes business sense, I enjoy it.

How can you merge what you do for a living with what you enjoy? As the business owner, you can engineer this, if you put your mind to it. Turn your business life into your leisure life, and you'll never work a day again! This may sound selfish, but as an entrepreneur you should be a little selfish. Create the business that not only delivers the most value to your clients, the most opportunity to grow for your team, but also the life that you want to live. This is your life, you only get one as far as I am aware, so make sure you spend it doing the things you want.

HAVE A PLAN AND STICK TO IT

Having last year completed Ironman Italy, I am currently in the heart of my training for Ironman Tallinn, which involves 2.4 miles of swimming, 112 miles of cycling and then the small issue of a 26.2 mile run to finish! I have lost count of the number of people who question how I can have the time to do the training required for this event, run a business and spend time with my family. It is all about planning.

This year I ran my first marathon in Brighton with three of the Efficient Portfolio team members. While this isn't a brilliant idea for the Ironman training, as the recovery is too long and risk of injury too high, I needed to have done it for the confidence. Imagine swimming and cycling for around nine hours and then embarking on your longest ever run. I needed to mentally have banked a marathon, so I knew I could do it again.

When chatting to a couple of the guys I swim with over a coffee one morning, they mentioned about the run/walk/run strategy created by Jeff Galloway. Like with most things, I went off and did some more research. Then I tried it, and it seemed to help me run further, with less pain both during and afterwards. This may sound like a strategy only used by the very slowest runners, but in my research I found someone called Mitch Phillips that had run a sub three-hour marathon with this approach. That was never going to be me, but I had mentally targeted sub four hours, so this seemed like a helpful approach to try.

As a result, for my training and for the marathon itself, I did a nine-minute run to one-minute walk strategy right from the start. This worked well, with the exception of the first couple of walking sections. The mental torment of walking just nine minutes into the marathon, with the crowd shouting things like "Come on mate, you can do it" was more difficult than I had anticipated. I just had to stare down at my watch to ignore them, in the hope that they realized it was part of the strategy. However, what it allowed me to do was to stick to nine minute miles throughout, which I knew would get me in under four hours. I finished in three hours and fifty-seven minutes, which I was really pleased with. The last few miles up hill into a headwind were tough, but I managed to maintain the same pace. The beauty of the run/walk/run strategy was that while everyone around me was slowing down, I was maintaining the same pace. I was also thinking, if this hurts now, imagine how it is going to feel having cycled 112 miles and swam 2.4 miles prior to starting, which is what the Ironman will bring.

Dan Sullivan of The Strategic Coach® Program talks about the four steps he's observed to create breakthrough results. He calls it 'The 4 C's Formula'®:[4]

COMMITMENT. First, you have to take a leap of faith and really commit to what you want to achieve – commit before you have crossed every 't' and dotted every 'i.' There's no doubt that this is scary.

COURAGE. Most people admire courage in others but don't like the experience themselves. In fact, this crucial step feels awful. You've committed yourself without having any proof that what you're going after is going to pay off.

CAPABILITY. Think back to one of your breakthroughs. Wasn't it the combination of making a commitment and going through a period requiring a lot of courage that created both the new capability and the new confidence?

CONFIDENCE. The new level of confidence you experience after a breakthrough is what gives you the ability to commit to an even bigger breakthrough and an even greater sense of confidence. And the process repeats itself.

By setting the goal to run a marathon, it was a leap of faith. Following making the commitment, I began to build up the courage to actually go and do it. I then started to research things like the run/walk/run strategy, so that I had the capability. That meant, on the day, I had the confidence to carry out the plan.

This is why the limitless life planner works so well. It forces you to make and revisit your commitments for a better future. As time passes you gain the courage, but you also start to find the resources that are going to give you the capability. This is what allowed me to write my first book. Initially, setting the commitment as a goal on the limitless life planner, I had no idea what the book would be about; I just knew I wanted to write a book. Over time, I found the courage to narrow down my subject and I ended up selecting the subject of retirement planning. As I did more research on the subject, I realized that retirement wasn't just about the money. It was about how people spent their time in retirement, and how they kept themselves fit, healthy and happy. I developed the capabilities to write about each of these areas. That gave me the confidence to get *The Dream Retirement* published in 2015.

The same applies to the one-page business plan. You are making the commitments for your business. As Dan Sullivan says, "Commitment ultimately leads to the confidence to achieve it."

MONDAY MORNING ROUTINE

The key to achieving your goals is to have a great system and to revisit it regularly. As I said earlier, "Losers have goals, winners have systems." The best way to do this is to build it into your The Happy Week. Build it into your schedule so that it happens, without fail, every week. For me, this is best done on a Monday morning, but that doesn't have to be the same for you. Monday, as you now know, is my team Focus Day®, ensuring they are all organized to achieve what we need to do that week. It is also the start of the week, when you are perhaps most likely to feel demotivated about being back in the office. As a result, it is a great time to set up an amazing week, as this will energize you for the week ahead.

Here is my Monday morning routine.

1. One-hour swim: a great way to energize yourself for the day ahead and clear out any cobwebs.

Once in the office, I then complete the following, in this order:

1. **ACHIEVEMENTS:** Essentially, a quick version of the best things exercise from *The Entrepreneurial Happiness Workbook*, I always start with a positive. I list the best personal and best business things that have happened in the last week. I do this in my limitless life planner.

2. **DIARY REVIEW:** Look at the week ahead to remind yourself what is happening when, so that you can identify the best times to do specific tasks, because we need to ensure we are only doing focus activities on Focus Days® where possible.

3. **GOAL REVIEW:** Read my month's limitless life planner goals. I'll also add anything relevant to these goals that needs to be done that week into my capture list.

4. **CAPTURE LIST:** By building my capture list on the limitless life planner, I have a list of things to do next week or month, so I'll review those and add them to my capture list. I'll also look at the week ahead and identify any other to do items and add them. This is your opportunity to get down any thoughts that have been banging around in your head. Don't do them now, just add them to the capture list.

5. **IDEAS ON THE MOVE:** From the notes on my phone I take any ideas that I have had during that week and either add them to my capture list or to the team planner to discuss at the brain trust meeting.

6. **SUCCESSFUL BUSINESS SCORECARD:** I'll review this document in detail, so I know what is happening in our business. Anything I spot that needs attention will go on the team planner to discuss at the brain trust meeting.

7. **TIME SYSTEM SPLIT:** I split my time into Free, Focus and Buffer Days. In order to ensure I am constantly improving my balance in these areas, I record how many I have that week. That way at the end of the year I can see what percentage of my time focused on each of these.

8. **CRUCIAL RESULTS:** As a result of reading my goals for the month, I ask myself what the most important things are I need to do this week to allow me to hit my goals. This ensures I am constantly moving towards my monthly, quarterly, yearly and, therefore, my lifetime goals, every single week.

9. **TRAINING PLAN:** In order to ensure I complete the required fitness training for that week, I ensure that every element of it is diarized. Typically, I have done this before I get to Monday morning, but this is my final opportunity to ensure the time I need for swimming, running and cycling is planned.

10. **MONTHLY/QUARTERLY GOALS:** On the first Monday of each month, and also the first week of each quarter, I will write my new monthly/quarterly goals to my capture list.

11. **ALLOCATE THE CAPTURE LIST:** Go through the capture list of jobs for the week ahead and allocate them to specific days. Group complementary activities together, so that you can work more effectively.

With every task, ask, "Could I delegate this to some-one else in my team? If so, how can I ensure I always delegate this going forwards?" If you can, move it to the team planner so that you have the follow up to make sure it gets done.

If you adopt and then adapt this approach to your life, you will be astonished at how much you can achieve. When you look back a few years from now at the goals that you are set-ting today, what seem like huge asks will more than likely have become easily realized achievements.

MAKING IT HAPPEN

"The only way to fail is to not try." – Charlie Reading

That last point is so important. It is very easy to get caught up in what you didn't do. If you have a goal to get to the stars and you fall short, you still hit the moon. By setting massive goals, whether you hit them all or not is not the important thing; it is about achieving so much more than you would have done otherwise. When you look back, you can beat yourself up for missing the bits you didn't do, or you can celebrate the success of what you did.

When I started writing this book, we had grown our new business levels by 50% in five of the last six years. In 2018, for quarters one, two and three, we were on track to do the same again. Then a combination of Brexit and falling markets led to an unusually quiet quarter four. As a result, we missed our 50% target. Now, we still grew our new business by over 30%, but we missed our target. I could have been down about missing that target, but I wasn't. I celebrated the success of growing by over 30%, which by many companies' standards is still amazing. And we celebrated that success as a team.

Recently, a good friend happened to pass comment on how happy the entire Efficient Portfolio team always seems to be.

Other friends tell me that they never have time to do the exercise they want, let alone find the time to train for an Ironman. Others tell me how lucky I am to be able to go cycling and diving in Miami as part of my working life.

I am not telling you this to impress you. I am telling you this to impress upon you that everything I have talked about in this book has had a tremendous impact on both my life and my business. This is from a dyslexic lad who struggled at school and generally lacked motivation for most things. I am not saying I have achieved the perfect balance, by any means. I am not saying I am making as much money as I would like to, as there is always room to improve. I am not saying my business runs perfectly, or that I absolutely love every minute of my working day. Life is not a game of perfection. What I am doing, however, is appreciating the success that a determination to create the best business and life possible has brought me so far. Clearly, there is always scope for everything to be better, but I am practising what I preach, and celebrating the 80% success rather than waiting for the 100% that will never come.

Without knowing the detail behind why my uncle Bill decided to take his own life, I do wonder if he was another example of someone who had mastered the success of achievement, but not the art of fulfilment. I certainly don't want to ever risk falling into that category. Happiness, after all, is in the eye of the beholder. It is vital to achieve what is important to you, but it is equally crucial to be content with the cards you are dealt. Perhaps if he'd been focused on continuing to grow as a person, and the contribution he could make to others, things might have been different.

Within this book are the secrets to my success so far. The exercises contain all the magic, because it isn't the principles I teach that will ultimately deliver the results, but rather the questions I ask. I encourage you to go to www.charliereading.com/EH to download the workbook and complete the exercises if you haven't done them already. If you have, congratulations on taking a massive step towards a better future, both financially and personally.

Complete in full the limitless life planner and, using the Monday morning routine, allow it to evolve every week into what will become your life's work. Utilize the team planner to ensure you get the best out of your team and you successfully delegate more. Diarize your quarterly leadership meetings, your weekly brain trust meetings and your monthly ENERGI meetings, because this will ensure everyone knows where they are going, what you are all doing and how it is getting done over a time frame that keeps you accountable. Build your successful business scorecard so you can keep track of your business and identify any future problems as early as possible.

Finally, accept that life is not a game of perfection. Doing all of these things at 80% is far better than trying to get any one area to 100%. Procrastination is a fear of starting, while perfectionism is a fear of finishing. Just accept that nothing will ever be perfect, and you will get a whole lot more done. It will allow you to market more, it will allow you to delegate more and, finally, it will allow you to be healthier and happier.

If you would like to know more about what we are up to, how you can create a better financial future or where you can attend one of our events, you can find out more at www.EfficientPortfolio.co.uk.

Remember, if you make the same decisions today as you made yesterday, you'll get the same results tomorrow as you got today. If you go ahead and make some significant decisions that will lead to significant changes in your life, then you too will reach entrepreneurial happiness.

4. Source: www.StrategicCoach.com.

CHAPTER SUMMARY

- This life is not a practice run. You need to step up and create the life you want now, not at some point in the future. You don't know when your time will be up.

- Protect your future plans through identifying key risks to you, your family and your business, so that when the unexpected happens, it doesn't derail the plan.

- Work doesn't have to be a chore. Work can be fun. Identify ways that you can merge work with the activities you enjoy, and 'you'll never work a day in your life.'

- Achieve more in your life by building a plan and executing it.

- Achieve more in less time by having an amazing Monday morning routine to allow you to delegate, delete or do the most impactful items on your to-do list.

- If you are going to take the island, you've got to burn the boats. Get on and do this, and you too can create entrepreneurial happiness.